Secret to Personal Health and Wellness Success

Master Health and Wellness

BEIRA BROWN

CONTENTS

INTRODUCTION

Yesterday I was clever, so I wanted to change the world. Today I am wise, so I am changing myself. —Rumi

The paradox of some secrets is that they're not really secrets at all. The answers can stare you right in the face, and you can still spend most of your life looking for them. When it comes to personal transformation, all the answers we seek are within us. This, however, doesn't mean that the journey to find these answers is easy. Why is that? What is it that stops us from achieving true personal health and wellness?

The first thing is an understanding of self-care. What is self-care if not "care for oneself?" Why is it so difficult to learn and practice self-care in our daily lives? There are a couple of reasons for this. One, self-care is not superficial. Most of the self-care and wellness industry today is built on "pampering yourself," which translates to spending money on expensive and even unnecessary products. I'm not saying that any of these products or routines can't be a part of your self-care practice. However, true self-care shouldn't stop there, as there are many more layers to it. What this also means is that true self-care can be way more un-comfortable and challenging than we think.

When we talk about self-care, we think of the ways we can appease ourselves in the present—either by in-dulging in our favorite foods or by spending the day shopping or getting pampered at a spa—instead of the ways in which we can improve our lives in concrete ways. When we talk about self-care, we rarely talk about discipline. When we talk about self-care, we hardly talk about showing up each day, even on (and especially on) the days we want to give up on ourselves. When we talk about self-care, we talk about the glamorous parts but not about the grim ones. We don't talk about self-care in terms of picking up after ourselves, cleaning up the messes we've made, and loving ourselves when we seem unlovable.

Self-care is both universal and personal. When we look at it from an industrial point of view, it seems that the solution to all our problems lies in a bottle of massage oil or in processed food. The truth, however, is that all of us are unique. The ways in which our souls respond to the world, both outside and within us, are different from each other. This means that we can only achieve true self-care when we begin to understand who we truly are. This doesn't mean that we need to do all the world in isolation, even though solitude can play a huge role in helping us understand ourselves. We need a community of people who can stand by our side as we discover ourselves, but the journey within can only be taken individually. This is the first pillar that this book stands on—giving you the courage to take care of yourselves in a holistic manner.

The second challenge that most of us face is a lack of mindfulness. Even though mindfulness can seem like a difficult thing to master, it's based on a simple principle. Most of us go through life either plagued by issues that we have no control over or worried about a future that we cannot predict. The past seems to weigh heavily on us, and the future looms ahead in a dark and uncertain manner. As a result, we forget to savor the only thing that we do have—the present. Mindfulness as a practice helps us immerse ourselves in whatever we're doing right now without judging ourselves for whatever we feel or think. It's not about running away from the difficult sensations; rather, it's about allowing them to wash over us. It's about acceptance and openness in whatever we do and whoever we become.

Once we begin to practice mindfulness, we can see our entire lives transforming from within. Mindfulness isn't limited to any one area of our lives, nor is it about disconnecting from our daily lives and retreating into a shell. In fact, it's about eating, sleeping, walking, and working mindfully. When we bring mindfulness into the equation, every activity we perform is touched with energy and purpose.

Once we've committed to a self-care routine that works for us and developed a mindfulness practice that helps us change our mindset and power our self-care practice, we're ready for the next stage of improving our health and our lives. Here, we often encounter the problem of wading through too much information without knowing where to start. When it comes to nutrition, exercise, rest, and mental health—there's so much advice and information available to us both online and offline that it can make our personal journeys confusing and difficult. Sometimes, this means that we end up following one diet after another, unable to form an eating routine that inherently makes sense to us. Other times, this means that we focus too much on one area of our lives, conveniently ignoring all the others. In both cases, it's our health that suffers.

The third pillar this book stands on is credible and relevant information that makes it easier for you to focus on your personal health and wellness journey without feeling overwhelmed or confused. This includes information related to nutrition, hydration, movement, rest, and mental health. Once you have all this information in front of you, you can make informed decisions about your own journey.

We can only truly achieve health and wellness when we get in touch with our own bodies, minds, and souls. So, this book will help you not only with the right kind of information on various topics, but it'll also help you develop your own intuition. It'll help you develop routines that work for you and that you can follow throughout your life. All of this will assist in making sustainable changes in your life. As difficult as it is to create change in our lives, it's even more challenging to maintain these changes over time. Hopefully, this book will give you the confidence to stick to the changes you make and create a life that you truly deserve.

Choosing Better Food Options

If we want to create a healthy lifestyle for ourselves, we need to start with nutrition. For most of us, food is about more than sustenance. It's related to our deepest relationships, emotions, and memories. Our relationship with food is at once personal and universal. Changing our food habits is one of the most challenging things that we can ever do. Before we start making better food choices for ourselves, let's understand why we need to do so.

Are We Facing a Nutritional Health Crisis?

Even before the COVID-19 pandemic, the world was staring at a health crisis of unprecedented proportions. For one, we're seeing a steady rise in the number of people—including children—being afflicted by different kinds of lifestyle diseases like heart disease and cancer. Two, the burden on our system is immense, both in terms of hospitalizations and lifelong medications. Overall, the quality of life has degraded for most people over the last few decades.

One of the major culprits for this is the crisis of malnutrition. While some areas of the world still face major challenges in getting regular access to clean and healthy food, the western world is faced with a unique problem. On the one hand, we're dealing with a culture of overeating, in which we regularly have more than the required amount of both calories and nutrients in our daily diet. On the other hand, we're also grappling with various kinds of nutritional deficiencies, which lead to a whole range of health issues. So, we're somehow consuming too much or too little at times. Poor nutrition has devastating effects not just on the individual but also on their family and community.

The Benefits of Nutrition

There are numerous benefits to eating nutritious food, such as

- It keeps your bones strong and healthy, and also helps build cells, tissues, and muscles. All of these together form the building blocks of the body and ensure that we can move well through the world. When our muscles face wear and tear, nutrients can help them recover much faster.

- Nutrition is also responsible for keeping our skin, eyes, teeth, and hair healthy. Adequate amounts of nutrition keep our skin luminous and protect it from inflammation, protect our teeth against decay and disease, and also provide strength to our hair.

- Nutrition can have a direct impact on our quality of life as well as our longevity. Not only does it boost our immune system and improve hormonal health, but it also protects us against a range of lifestyle diseases such as cancer, stroke, type 2 diabetes, and heart disease.

- When we eat nutritious food, we ensure that our gut remains healthy. This helps the body in its digestive processes, which means it can absorb more nutrition from whatever you consume. Good gut health also has an impact on your overall physical, mental, and emotional health.

- It's a fallacy that we need to eat less or restrict ourselves immensely to lose weight or even to maintain weight loss. Depending on your current calorie consumption, you might need to reduce your calorie intake for some time, but that doesn't mean you have to go hungry. In fact, the healthiest foods leave you feeling full and help curb your hunger pangs. This is because they're nutritionally dense.

- For expectant and new mothers, nutrition is especially important, both for their and their child's health. During the breastfeeding stage, it's vital to eat nutritional food so that your baby gets everything that is essential for its growth and development.

- Having nutritional food can ensure that a child develops mentally and physically during their formative years.

Nutritional Recommendations for a Healthy Life

Most of us have heard about the importance of a balanced diet in our lives. What exactly is a balanced diet? Simply put, a balanced diet is one that contains the right amount of macronutrients (fats, proteins, and carbohydrates), micronutrients (vitamins and minerals), and water to keep ourselves healthy. These foods make sure that our bodies have the energy they need and the ability to perform their functions well.

Most of us don't enjoy a balanced diet. Our food is either extremely rich or deficient in one or more of the macronutrients. Also, micronutrients are usually needed in very small quantities, but they're only provided by specific foods. This means that we might miss out on these crucial nutrients if we're not paying attention to what we consume.

In 2020, the World Health Organization issued certain guidelines to ensure better dietary practices:

- In general, adults should have at least five portions, or 400 g, of fruits and vegetables in their daily diet. This would mean that each meal should contain fruits and vegetables. If possible, we should try to substitute processed snacks with fruits and vegetables as well.

- For both health and environmental reasons, it's much better to eat fruits and vegetables that are organically grown and locally sourced.

- A good diet should be diverse. This means that you should have enough carbs, proteins, and fats from various sources. This diversity will also ensure that your diet is rich in fiber, minerals, and vitamins.

- We should consume more non-starchy vegetables rather than starchy ones like sweet potatoes and cassava.

- Most adults need to cut their sugar and salt intake drastically to reduce their risk of lifestyle diseases.

- When it comes to fats, it's important to focus on healthy fats instead of trans and saturated fats. For example, about 30% of your daily calorie intake should come from fats, of which less than 10% should come from saturated fats and less than 1% from trans fats. Some common sources of saturated fats are cheese, ghee, butter, lard, coconut oil, palm oil, and fatty meats. Trans fats are found in the meat of animals such as goats, sheep, and cows, as well as in many processed foods such as chips, cookies, pies, pizzas, and even some cooking oils and spreads. You can reduce your consumption of unhealthy fats by choosing lean, white, and unprocessed meats whenever possible. You can also choose to cook with oils that are rich in unsaturated fats, such as sunflower, safflower, canola, olive, corn, and soybean oils. Other healthy sources of unsaturated fats are avocado, fish, nuts, and seeds. Another simple way to reduce the amount of fats you consume regularly is by grilling, roasting, boiling, or steaming your foods instead of deep-frying them.

- For those who are expecting or new mothers, it's important to ensure that their infants are getting the nutrition they require. The first two years of their lives can be extremely crucial for their proper growth and development and can also create an internal environment that protects them against the onset of various diseases later in life. For this, it's important to give them all the nutrients they need in the first six months of their life through breastfeeding. After six months, breastfeeding should continue till they reach two years of age, and solid food that is rich in nutrients should also be started.

Taking Supplements as Part of Your Diet

In the absence of a balanced diet, we might be missing out on various essential nutrients that benefit our bodies. In these situations, we might consider taking certain supplements to prevent deficiencies and health issues. That being said, there are certain things to keep in mind before you consider taking supplements. One, make sure that you're not taking too many supplements in your diet. In other words, don't rely on supplements to fulfill all your nutritional requirements. As much as possible, let your diet take care of your needs.

Two, do your research before taking any supplements. Always consult with your primary physician and ask them for trusted recommendations. Even though the Food and Drug Administration (FDA) has started to regulate supplements, the procedures are not as strict as they are for pharmaceutical drugs. This means that some of these supplements might be neither safe nor effective. Also, our bodies react differently to different foods as well as drugs. So, what works for someone else may not work for you.

Some of the most common supplements that you can take for better health are probiotics, multivitamins, magnesium, and fish oil.

Fish oil supplements help fulfill our requirements for omega-3 fatty acids. Since these compounds are extremely effective in fighting inflammation, they're important for maintaining our immunity, as well as improving our cardiovascular, respiratory, and mental health. Adequate amounts of omega-3 fatty acids can also positively impact your bone and muscular health. Some of the best sources of omega-3 fatty acids are anchovies, sardines, herring, salmon, mackerel, and oysters. If you're vegetarian, you can eat walnuts, chia seeds, flax seeds, and soybeans to fulfill your requirements. However, if your diet is extremely deficient in these compounds, it might be a good idea to take cod liver oil supplements in your diet.

Another nutrient that most of us are deficient in is vitamin D. Healthy levels of vitamin D help in maintaining bone and muscular health, normal blood pressure levels, and healthy immune responses. One of the best sources of vitamin D is regular sun exposure. The problem is most of us live in areas where we don't get enough regular sunlight. Even if we do, our current lifestyles make it difficult for us to get regular sun exposure. When your vitamin D levels become dangerously low, it can lead to physical injuries and respiratory problems. So, it might be a good idea to supplement your diet with vitamin D after consulting your doctor.

Apart from vitamin D, some of the other common deficiencies include vitamin C, vitamin B12, and vitamin B6. When it comes to minerals, many people are unable to meet their requirements for magnesium through diet, which leads to fatigue, irritability, muscle cramps, blood pressure and heart problems, and inability to metabolize vitamin D properly. One of the main reasons that people suffer from these deficiencies is because their meals are rich in processed foods, especially meats, and deficient in fruits and vegetables. Also, some people might consume too much alcohol, which can also lead to a deficiency in magnesium. In some cases, certain medical conditions, such as diabetes, might also lead to such problems. Again, your focus should be on improving your regular diet before you take supplements for these micronutrients.

With the growing interest in gut health, there's a greater emphasis on taking probiotic and prebiotic supplements in our diet. While probiotics are the "good" bacteria that live in the gut and improve our gut health, prebiotics are the foods that help these good bacteria to grow. So, a combination of both can lead to a healthy gut microbiome, which can lead to better physical, mental, and emotional health.

While there are supplements available for our probiotic and prebiotic needs, there are many foods that can also help us in this endeavor. For example, fermented foods such as kimchi, sauerkraut, kefir, miso, unsweetened yogurt, buttermilk, and kombucha are all excellent sources of probiotics. Similarly, foods such as garlic, leeks, onions, asparagus, bananas, oats, barley, apples, and flaxseeds are great sources of prebiotics.

Even if you end up taking supplements after consulting your doctor, make sure that you look for natural sources of different minerals and vitamins in your diet.

The Importance of Reading Food Labels

The FDA has made it mandatory for a Nutrition Facts label to be provided by manufacturers on most packaged foods and beverages. While fresh foods might not have a label present on them, you can always go to the US Department of Agriculture (USDA) website to get the nutritional information required.

If you don't know what you're looking for, food labels can leave you confused. So, there are some things that you need to keep in mind when it comes to them:

- The most important things to understand are the number of servings per container and the average serving size that is listed on the label. While the average serving size gives you an idea of the amount of food that people typically consume, the number of servings will give you a sense of the number of calories you consume each time you eat a particular food product.

- The other important term is % daily value (DV). This tells you about the amount of a particular nutrient that is usually a part of your diet. In general, if a food product contains less than 5% DV of a particular nutrient, it's considered low in that nutrient. Similarly, a product that contains more than 20% of a particular nutrient is high in that nutrient. You should consider a few more things before you decide whether a particular product is healthy for you or not. For one, your total calorie intake in a day will likely differ from others. So, you might need a product with a higher % DV than recommended. Also, a product that is higher in fiber content will likely be a better choice than one higher in sugar. So, it's important to understand what your dietary needs are, what you're lacking, and what you need to reduce before you make decisions based on % DV.

- One thing that food labels might not always help you with is in understanding whether a product is safe to consume or not. This is because these dates are not mandated by the FDA and are only voluntarily added by manufacturers. Still, there are certain terms that you can look out for. For example, if a product has a "best if used by" date, it will have the best quality of flavor before then. The same goes for "use by" date, though this is more affirmative in nature. The "sell by" date is one by which the retailer should sell their product and is typically used for products with a shorter shelf-life, such as eggs, milk, and poultry. In general, you should shop from places where food products are sold and restocked regularly. This will ensure that your product hasn't been languishing in a store for too long. When it comes to bread, milk, eggs, fish, and poultry, pay special attention to their quality and freshness.

There are some other terms that you might need to understand clearly before deciding to buy a particular food product. For example, a food can only be called organic if it has been grown or bred (in the case of animals) without synthetic fertilizers, chemical pesticides, radiation, hormones, or antibiotics. If the animals are fed inorganic or chemically-laced foods before being killed, they're not considered organic. While organic foods are certainly healthier in terms of their quality, they might still be calorie-dense and nutrient-poor.

When it comes to low-fat, low-calorie, or low-carb foods, you need to understand their total nutrient profile before considering whether they're worth consuming. For example, a low-carb food could be extremely high in unhealthy fats. Similarly, a low-calorie product might be deficient in important nutrients. Also, the average serving size and the number of servings of these foods matter. For example, if you eat more servings of a low-calorie product, you might still be consuming a higher number of overall calories. The same goes for foods that are labeled "light." Simply because they're lower in calories or fat as compared to their original versions, it doesn't mean that they're necessarily healthier.

Another popular term that most food manufacturers use is "multigrain." Essentially, a food rich in multi grains simply implies that more than one grain has been used to create it. While this can be good in terms of diversity, the quality of the grains is also important. For example, if most or all of the grains used are refined rather than whole, you're still consuming something that is harmful to your health.

In the beginning, it can get a bit overwhelming to read each food label and understand what that means for your health. However, once you get used to it, it'll become second nature to you. Moreover, this practice of truly understanding what goes into your food will ensure that you don't take your nutrition for granted.

In the next chapter, we'll discuss ways to regulate our consumption of foods that are low in nutrition.

LESS IS MORE

The standard American diet (SAD) that most of us follow is extremely poor in nutritional value. A major part of this diet contains highly processed junk food, which is harmful to our mental and physical health. In this chapter, we'll discuss the main issues that arise with such diets and also understand how to make our diets healthier.

Salt

The western diet is notoriously high in salt content. Perhaps the worst part is that most of us aren't even aware of the amount of salt we consume daily because most of it is hidden in the foods that we commonly eat. According to the World Health Organization

(WHO), the average person consumes about 9-12 g of sodium in salt each day, which is more than twice the daily recommended limit of less than 5 g. On the other hand, our consumption of potassium might be too low (less than 3.5 g daily). When you combine excessive levels of sodium intake with dangerously low levels of potassium intake, you're at a higher risk for diseases like stroke, heart attack, kidney disease, and heart failure because of high blood pressure.

The FDA also regulates how much salt you should be consuming daily. You can understand this using %DV as a guideline. %DV is useful in telling us how much of a particular nutrient we're consuming in our regular diet. For example, if you're consuming more than 20% DV of sodium per serving in your diet, your diet is very high in sodium. You should aim for a DV of less than 5% or 2300 mg per day.

The challenge that most of us face is in recognizing the common sources of excessive sodium consumption. What are some things you can do about this? If you reduce your intake of highly processed foods, including processed meats, savory snacks, soups, and bread, you'll have reduced your sodium intake. Another simple way to reduce our sodium intake is by reducing the amount of food we consume daily. While this might not be easy to do, the least we can do is switch from foods rich in sodium to those that aren't.

One of the best ways of gaining control over your nutrients is to prepare the food yourself. I understand that this is not always possible, but you can try to minimize your dependence on dining out or takeout as much as you can. The entire process starts when you shop for groceries. You need to be on the lookout for pre-packaged snacks and other items that you might casually pick up while shopping. It's also important to consider what kind of condiments and sauces you're choosing to cook with. Most of them have much higher sodium content than we need in our daily lives. It's always better to create your own spice mixes and blends using herbs so that you can regulate the amount of salt you're consuming. In fact, one of the best ways to control your consumption of sugar is to learn to work with pepper. If you don't like your food too spicy, you can control the amount of pepper you use, but even a little bit goes a long way in making your food taste better without compromising on health. Of course, if you have an inflamed gut lining, you might need to be careful about the kind of spices you use.

When it comes to snacks, it's a great idea to start preparing your own with different kinds of nuts, seeds, and even veggie sticks. Since processed food can be one of the major culprits when it comes to our sodium consumption, it's best to buy fresh food whenever possible. This goes for the meat you eat, as well as the vegetables you buy. For example, certain canned foods can contain high amounts of sodium in order to preserve them. If you do end up buying foods that contain sodium, you should always rinse them before you cook them, as that can get rid of at least some of the sodium content.

If you do end up eating at a restaurant, it's up to you to look for ways to curb your sodium consumption. For example, wherever possible, try to avoid getting dressings or sauces on the side. Also, you can fill some parts of your plate with salads so that you consume less of the cooked food you've ordered. In general, try to increase your consumption of fruits and vegetables because they're rich in potassium. An increased intake of potassium can counter the intake of sodium.

One of the reasons why it can be tough to understand whether a particular food product is high in sodium is because even foods that don't taste salty can contain lots of sodium content. If we read food labels, we'll get more information about the ingredients that go into each product that we buy, as well as the number of ingredients used. According to the FDA rules, the list of ingredients follows a descending order. So, if you find that salt is one of the first few ingredients used in a product, there's a good chance that it has way more salt than you need. Also, it's important to pay attention to the serving size of each product. For example, if the recommended serving size of a condiment is 3-4 tablespoons, you need to see how much that would amount to in terms of grams and what would be its %DV in your diet. You may use more or less of the product in your cooking, which will influence the amount of sodium you consume.

When reading food labels, you might come across certain terms that confuse you. After all, it can be difficult to understand the difference between low sodium and reduced sodium, or even between low sodium and very low sodium. Let's clarify what these terms mean. If you see a product that calls itself unsalted or "no salt added," it means that there was no salt added to it during processing. However, it might still contain more sodium than recommended.

Then there are products that come in different versions. For example, you might come across a "lightly salted" or "light in sodium" version of a product. This means that the particular product contains at least 50% less sodium than the original product. Similarly, a "reduced sodium" version contains at least 25% less sodium than the original.

If something is sodium-free or salt-free, it has less than 5 mg of sodium per serving. Very low sodium means that the product contains less than 35 mg of sodium per serving, while low sodium refers to 140 mg or less of sodium per serving.

While it might take some time for you to get used to lower levels of sodium in your food, being aware of your own eating patterns can go a long way in helping you change your habits.

Sugar

The amount of sugar we consume has also risen dramatically over the last few decades. The thing is, while many foods contain natural sugars, it's the added sugar in our foods and beverages that causes maximum harm to our overall health. Think about it—there are many foods that are rich in glucose, fructose, or other sugars. For example, most fruits contain sugar. So do foods that are high in starch content. In fact, there's a scale known as the glycemic index (GI) scale, which helps us understand how different foods (rich in carbs) affect our blood glucose levels. This is because carbohydrates are broken down into glucose by the body and are then absorbed into the bloodstream.

Since we already get more than enough sugar from whole foods, we don't really need refined or added sugar that is abundantly present in processed foods. How does too much sugar affect us? An excess of sugar can have a negative effect on almost every part of our body—including our teeth, skin, kidneys, liver, and heart. It can affect our blood sugar levels to the extent that it causes type 2 diabetes, which can be dangerous for the health of most of our organs.

Sugar can also lead to lethargy, foggy thinking, and irritability. One of the reasons is that excess consumption of added sugar can cause a dramatic rise in our blood sugar levels, which is quickly followed by a sugar crash. This crash can lead to both increased hunger and cravings, interrupted sleep cycles, and low moods. So, added sugar in your diet can harm your mental and emotional health as well.

Did you know that sugar plays an important role in your gut health? Our gut microbiome can be negatively impacted by too much sugar, as this causes an overgrowth of harmful bacteria in the gut. When our gut health is compromised, it can affect our physical, mental, and emotional health in many ways.

As with salt, we probably don't understand how much added sugar we consume each day. To better understand our consumption, let's first know that one teaspoon of sugar is roughly equivalent to four grams. According to the American Heart Association (AHA), adult women don't need more than 24 grams, and adult men don't need more than 36 grams of sugar each day. Think about it, that's less than six teaspoons for women and less than nine teaspoons for men. Most of us consume much more than that as part of our daily intake. According to WHO, the average American has 17 teaspoons of sugar daily, which is almost twice the limit for men, and almost thrice the limit for women.

While different health institutions have their own guidelines for daily sugar intake, most of them agree on keeping it below 50 grams, which roughly translates to 200 calories on a 2,000-calorie diet (Dietary Guidelines for Americans 2020-2025). Not only do most of us consume too much sugar, but most of that sugar is in the form of added sugar.

This might be concerning, but you can also understand it this way. If you learn to spot the main sources of added sugar in your diet, you'll become more conscious of your sugar consumption. Again, the best way to do this is to learn to read food labels. Fortunately for us, the Nutrition Facts label that is approved by the FDA has become much clearer to read. For one, it's mandatory for manufacturers to state both "Total sugars" and "Added sugars" on the label. This can help you differentiate between foods that are rich in natural sugars, such as unsweetened yogurt or milk, and those that have excessive amounts of added sugars in them, such as various kinds of processed foods.

Second, you should look at %DV for sugar, just as you did with salt. While 5% DV per serving is considered low in added sugar, 20% DV per serving is considered high. In general, keeping your added sugar intake to 10% of your total diet can help maintain your overall health.

Third, make a list of the foods that usually contain huge amounts of added sugar. These are the foods you need to avoid when you're shopping for groceries. For example, sugary beverages are usually the biggest culprit when it comes to increased sugar intake. There are a couple of reasons why they're problematic. One, they don't contain much besides sugar. Two, it's much easier to consume extra calories in liquid form. After all, it is easier to gulp down an entire bottle of your favorite soda than it is to eat a whole medium-sized cake, right? Three, serving sizes become tricky when it comes to liquids. Depending on the manufacturer, every beverage might have a different serving size, which means that even a drink that's lower in calories might end up increasing your overall calorie intake if you consume it in greater amounts as compared to a higher-calorie one.

The FDA has asked manufacturers to be careful when listing serving sizes and letting consumers know how much they usually consume. As things stand, however, this can still be consuming for most consumers.

The other main (hidden) sources of added sugar are sauces, condiments, and dips of all kinds. While there are alternatives to these sauces in the market if you look hard enough, most of our favorite foods that we use to jazz up our meals contain unhealthy amounts of added sugar. It becomes trickier to understand this because these aren't foods we would usually call sweet. So, carefully reading the food labels is all we've got. The same goes for breakfast cereals. While many cereal manufacturers claim that these cereals are fortified with fiber, antioxidants, and certain important vitamins and minerals, it doesn't take away from the fact that they're also extremely high in added sugar. So, whatever benefits your children or you might be getting from making these a part of your breakfast routine are undermined by the amount of sugar you consume in the process.

It's clear that we need to take matters into our own hands to protect ourselves and our families from consuming too much sugar daily. Here are some things you can keep in mind:

- Look at products where sugar is one of the first five ingredients on the list. In these cases, you can be sure that the product has too much added sugar, and you can safely eliminate them from your diet.

- If you don't find the word "sugar" on the list, don't assume that it's not present. Instead, look for other words that essentially mean the same thing. These include corn syrup, high fructose corn syrup, molasses, maple syrup, malt syrup, fructose, corn sweetener, evaporated cane juice, honey, and so on.

- Try to drink plain water instead of soda and other carbonated drinks to quench your thirst. You might feel like these drinks refresh you at first, but they usually leave you more thirsty after some time. If you find plain water too boring, you can always add lemon or cucumber to add some freshness without any extra calories. Even fruit juices should be consumed as little as possible. Pre-packed ones are a no-no because they barely contain actual fruit. Even the ones at home are devoid of fiber, which means you're essentially drinking sugar. When it comes to beverages such as tea and coffee, keep them to a minimum because they have caffeine. Whenever possible, go for herbal teas, which are full of antioxidants, and keep the added sugar to a minimum. Some other beverages to consider are unsweetened kombucha and buttermilk, both of which are fermented and rich in probiotics. If you're traveling, try to keep a filled water bottle with you as much as you can. This way, when you feel thirsty, you'll be able to drink water instead of picking up the first packaged drink you get at a store.

- One thing to remember with sugar is that our bodies don't need as much sugar as we give them, which also means that our bodies can very easily live without sugar. In fact, we probably taste too much sugar in our diet. So, if we start replacing most of the sweet foods we have with either their unsweetened versions or with foods that have different predominant tastes, we'll get used to those tastes faster than we think. What I'm trying to tell you is that cutting down your consumption of sugar might be easier than you think. For example, a healthy alternative to breakfast cereal might be oats and plain yogurt, with a topping of fruits for some natural sweetness. Similarly, if you want to add some flair to your meals without having to rely on sugar-laden sauces and dips, you can make your own using herbs and whole spices. It's easier than you think, and it's much healthier, as herbs and spices are plant-based foods that are rich in antioxidants.

- If you have a sweet tooth, you might find it challenging to kick the habit immediately. What you can do is control your portion size when eating such foods. This advice applies to any food that you're trying to consume less of. In fact, it's a great idea to fill your plate with different kinds of foods and try to eat healthier foods before you eat others. For example, if you eat a salad before your meal, you're less likely to eat a lot of grains or grain-based meals. Similarly, if you have nuts, yogurt, and fruit before you go for a dessert, you'll automatically consume less than you want to.

Once you reduce your dependence on added sugar, you might be able to appreciate the natural sweetness that is found in fruits, many vegetables, and whole grains.

Protein

Protein is one of three macronutrients (fats, proteins, and carbohydrates) that are essential for good health. We need adequate amounts of all three, as well as minerals and vitamins, in a balanced diet. The thing is, proteins are usually overhyped when it comes to their role in our health. Don't get me wrong; proteins are really important for our cellular and muscular health. In fact, proteins make up most of the body, which is why if we're dealing with poor skin or hair health, we're usually asked to look into our protein intake.

Proteins are especially important for people who exercise regularly and those who do intense strength training. Not only do proteins help in repairing your body after workouts, but they also help in building muscle. This is why protein supplements have become extremely popular among fitness enthusiasts.

However, you might be surprised to know that, according to the Dietary Guidelines for Americans (2020-2025), most of us are eating more protein than our body needs. In fact, even athletes and bodybuilders may not need more protein than they're regularly eating. How much protein do we need on average? Based on research, the recommended dietary allowance (RDA) for proteins has been set at 0.8 g per kg of body weight. In general, this amounts to anywhere between 10-35% of your daily calorie intake. Of course, this number increases depending on your life stage and lifestyle. For example, if you exercise regularly and want to build muscle, you might need to increase your intake to 1.1-1.5 kg of your body weight. Similarly, as you grow older, your muscles lose mass naturally, so you might need to increase your intake to make up for it.

However, in most cases, consuming more than 2 g of protein per kg of body weight is considered too much and might lead to a host of problems. For one, protein that doesn't get metabolized immediately leads to fat storage. So, too much protein can lead to health issues similar to excessive fat consumption. Also, too much protein can put pressure on the kidneys. For people who suffer from any kind of kidney disease, excessive protein consumption can lead to further complications as the kidneys might not be able to remove all the waste accumulated in the blood.

You also need to consider what your sources of protein are. The best sources of protein are fish, most kinds of seafood, egg whites, white (lean) meat, low-fat dairy, and plant-based foods such as nuts, seeds, soy, lentils, and beans. However, many people tend to eat foods that are high in unhealthy fats when trying to increase their protein intake. Also, there's a tendency to get proteins from supplements and powders, which isn't always a good idea. Most supplements aren't regulated by the FDA, which might make them dangerous. Even if they're safe, they might not be particularly effective, especially because supplements cannot replace a balanced diet. At most, these supplements will contain protein, which you can get from a healthy diet anyway. Also, a healthy diet will contain healthy fats, carbohydrates, vitamins, and minerals.

If you do choose supplements for your protein intake, make sure that it has no sugar or is lower than 5 g of sugar. Also, it should not contain trans fats and limited amounts of saturated fats, if at all. Make sure that your overall calorie consumption from these supplements is also low. According to the RDA, eating about 15-30 g of protein per meal should take care of your daily requirements. You can consume this much simply by adding one source of dairy, like milk or yogurt, and meat, eggs, or soy in small quantities.

Ultra-Processed Food

One of the biggest issues with our diets these days is the amount of highly processed foods we eat on a regular basis. These foods are chemically altered in such a way that they barely contain any nutrients that are naturally present in whole foods. Not only are they deficient in healthy fats, carbohydrates (especially fiber), proteins, and micronutrients, but they're also full of chemical additives that are harmful to our health.

Think of the foods and drinks you casually pick up from the nearest store, or those that you stock up your refrigerator and pantry with for snacking purposes, or even the foods that you might order when you don't feel like cooking and want something cheap and convenient. The thing is, because these foods are accessible, most people don't think twice before consuming them regularly. These include fast food, cakes, cookies, soft drinks, savory snacks like chips, and even cold cuts, frozen meats, and hot dogs.

Why are these foods so irresistible? Why are they always delicious and almost addictive? Why don't they change their form even after a long amount of time? The answers to all these questions are interconnected. It's because these foods don't exist in nature and are instead manufactured in factories to be sold to a large number of unsuspecting people (especially children).

In recent times, the amount of research into the harmful effects of such foods has increased. In 2019, two notable studies were published in *BMJ*, which looked at the connection between the overconsumption of ultra-processed foods and the rising cases of lifestyle diseases. One study concluded that regular consumption of highly processed foods (more than four servings daily) increased the risk of all-cause mortality (disease due to any cause) by a whopping 62%. What's more, with each additional serving of ultra-processed foods, the mortality rate increased by 18% (Rico-Campà et al., 2019).

According to a longitudinal study conducted in France between 2009-2018, it became clear that a 10% increase in consumption of ultra-processed foods could increase the risk for cardiovascular diseases by 12%, cerebrovascular diseases by 11%, and coronary heart disease by 13% (Srour et al., 2019).

Therefore, it becomes extremely important for us to limit our consumption of these foods and include more whole foods in our diet. Essentially, whole foods are anything that can be found in nature. This includes various kinds of plant-based foods such as nuts, seeds, fruits, vegetables, and even animal products that are derived as naturally as possible. When going for eggs or poultry, make sure that they're free-range. This ensures that the animals have been allowed to roam outdoors for a major part of their time. Similarly, when buying fish such as salmon, make sure they're wild instead of farmed. You might think that it's taxing to create food from scratch, but this is a common misconception. In fact, most foods are beneficial to us when they're eaten raw or when they're cooked as little as possible. So, not only don't you need to make elaborate efforts for your meals, but it's also better if you don't spend too much time cooking your food.

Also, it might seem challenging at first to move from a diet rich in processed foods (the food companies make sure of this) to one that contains whole foods. However, our taste buds adapt really quickly, and when we see our bodies and minds loving this change, we'll get the motivation needed to stick to our new diet.

In the last two chapters, we've understood why it's important to eat nutritious food. Let's now move on to the importance of movement for better health.

AS ACTIVE AS POSSIBLE

Just as diet is important for a healthy life, so too is proper and regular exercise. When you exercise regularly, you improve your mental, physical, and emotional health. There are a few misconceptions when it comes to exercise. You don't need to join a gym or take part in an expensive program to become physically fit or active. Of course, training under a good teacher does help immensely, especially in the beginning. However, it's much more important to understand our body's needs and take care of them in a way that minimizes injury and maximizes health. This might take some time to get right, but being active is one of the best things you can do for your overall health and longevity.

Benefits of Physical Activity

Let's look at some common benefits of regular physical activity.

Healthy Weight Loss and Weight Management

If you want to lose weight, one of the most effective ways to do so is to burn more calories than you're consuming each day. It's extremely important to eat nutritious foods that are low in calories so that you achieve a calorie deficit. However, starving yourself isn't a good idea. Also, some highly nutritious foods might also be higher in calories. So, it's a good idea to engage in some physical activity each day. If you want to work under a certified trainer, go for it.

Even if you don't feel like hitting the gym, you can achieve most of your fitness goals by engaging in moderate physical activities as well. Even a brisk walk for thirty minutes each day can bring you much closer to your weight loss goals. Of course, you might need to engage in more intense physical activity if you want to lose weight instead of simply maintaining it. It's important to remember that each of our bodies is different, so our needs might also differ. Also, sustainable weight loss can rarely be achieved without making adequate changes to your diet.

Protection Against Certain Diseases

Lifestyle diseases are on the rise in the US and in most of the world. One of the major reasons for this, apart from poor diet, is a rise in sedentary lifestyles. As more of us spend our time chained to our desks and staring at screens, our bodies have become more susceptible to certain cancers, cardiovascular diseases, and diabetes. Also, inflammatory and autoimmune diseases have become much more common among young people.

Regular physical activity can help us in combating these diseases. For example, regular exercise can help improve our heart health by fighting against the buildup of "bad" cholesterol and keeping our blood pressure in check. Regular exercise can also help in preventing metabolic syndrome and type 2 diabetes. Metabolic syndrome occurs when we're dealing with high blood pressure, high blood sugar, high levels of bad cholesterol, and excessive weight gain.

Also, when you engage in regular exercise, you reduce your chances of developing certain cancers, such as lung, stomach, kidney, colon, breast, esophagus, bladder, endometrium, and bladder cancer. In most cases, physical exercise can also help us in recovering faster after a disease. Of course, you should consult with your doctor before committing to an exercise regime if you're unwell.

Increase in Physical Strength and Vitality

Some people might be worried about engaging in physical activity because they lack strength or stamina. The good news is you can start out slow and watch as your body becomes stronger each day. One of the best ways to do this is by engaging in regular strength training activities. Strength training helps build your muscle strength and also provides protection against injury. This is especially important for older people, who lose strength in their bones, muscles, and joints, and are extremely susceptible to hurting themselves by falling down. This is why it's also important to work on your balance as you grow older. Some of the best ways to improve balance are yoga and tai chi.

Also, when you engage in regular physical exercise, you boost your energy levels. This is because your heart and lung function improve considerably, especially through cardio exercises. Also, exercise increases the amount of oxygen that reaches your tissues, which can make you feel more energized. Regular exercise also helps build your endurance levels, which means that you don't get tired as easily as before.

Better Mental and Emotional Health

If you think that physical activity can only affect your physical health, think again. Exercise has a positive impact on our mental and emotional health. Regular exercise is often associated with the release of feel-good hormones such as dopamine and oxytocin. In fact, it also influences the regulation of the sleep hormone melatonin. Therefore, it can help in reducing stress, anxiety, and even depression in some cases. Also, if you spend some time exercising outdoors, these benefits might be compounded.

In fact, regular exercise can also help in managing chronic pain, which leads to an enhanced quality of life. Physical activities can also help in improving our sleep quality and sex life, both of which contribute to better mental and emotional health.

Now that we know the benefits of exercising regularly, let's discuss how to stick to a regular fitness regime.

Getting Started With Exercise

If you've not exercised for a long time, or if you're simply not used to a lot of physical activity, it can be a little intimidating to start your journey. However, there are a few things that can help you make the most of this new lifestyle.

First, it's always a good idea to get yourself assessed before you start a fitness regimen. Of course, activities such as walking (especially at a slow or moderate pace) should be fine for most people, irrespective of their age or physical condition. Still, you should try to understand what your current fitness levels are so that you have an idea of how far and how fast you can go. For this, you can record your weight, body fat composition, and body mass index (BMI) to begin with. You can also assess your pulse rate after a short run or walk. Similarly, a good measure of your fitness is the amount of time it takes for you to walk or run a certain distance. You can also get a sense of your body's flexibility and balance before starting your routine.

After this, you need to set certain goals for yourself. You could set a weight loss goal, but I think it's much more effective to focus on creating a routine at this time. This is because it can take some time for results to show, and you need to stay motivated till they do.

So, you could set yourself a goal of walking a certain number of miles each day or of spending half an hour doing yoga. A good idea is to set goals that are extremely personal and meaningful to you. For example, you could decide that you'll run a marathon with your partner or friend at the end of a year. Or, you could aim to play with your kids throughout the weekend without getting tired.

Only you can create a fitness program that works for you. If you're completely new to this, you can ask for help from a trainer. It's a good idea to create a routine that takes care of balance, flexibility, endurance, and strength. Also, it's more important that you show up for yourself as regularly as possible instead of doing something extremely intense for a few days and then discontinuing your practice. So, even half an hour of exercise every day can make an enormous difference when you're starting out. The good thing about exercise is—the more you stick with it, the more you'll fall in love with it. That's because your mind will crave the "high" it gets every time you walk, run, do yoga, or hit the gym.

Depending on your fitness levels and physical condition, you might need to go easy on certain kinds of exercises. In general, however, it's a good idea to combine cardio with weight training in a week. Some good cardio exercises for beginners include walking, jogging, biking, and swimming. Strength training can be done by using your own body weight or by using physical weights to lift and train with. Start slowly and then build your routine, depending on your stamina.

You should spend some time investing in good quality equipment. For example, you should invest in shoes that are good for walking and running, and that can protect you from injury on different terrains. Similarly, if you're investing in weights or resistance bands for strength training at home, make sure they're of good quality and are recommended by trainers and fitness enthusiasts. It could be a bit expensive in the beginning, but good equipment ensures that you continue your fitness journey without any setbacks.

There are some things you should keep in mind when starting a fitness routine:

- While it's understandable that you're enthusiastic and raring to go when you start, try to start as slowly as possible. This is because your body might not be used to regular physical activity and might be susceptible to injury. Also, if you put in too much effort in the beginning, you might get fatigued very soon, which will prevent you from being consistent with your routine. Your body will let you know when you're ready to take the next step in your program.

- Always allow time for adequate rest and recovery. You might not understand the need for it in the beginning, especially if you're young. However, proper recovery is important not just to prevent serious injuries but also to advance on your fitness journey. Your body will hit a plateau if you keep pushing it without giving it time to rest and recover.

- Get creative with your fitness routine. As motivated as you might be, it can get boring to stick to the same program each day or week. So, once you've got the basics right, try to incorporate different elements into your exercise routine. Make it as fun for yourself as possible. It's even better if you can get a friend to accompany you on this journey, as you can keep each other accountable and also enjoy the process. While routine is important, it doesn't hurt to surprise yourself once in a while.

- Always pay attention to your body. Your body's always trying to communicate with you. If you feel uneasy after a workout, take a rest. If you feel extremely fatigued after a fitness routine, get yourself assistance. If your body's asking you to go easy or stop at any point of the routine, listen to it.

- It's a good idea to become more active in your life in general. This means that you can make small tweaks to your daily schedule and incorporate more movement into it. If you can, you could take the stairs instead of the elevator once in a while. If your work supports a sedentary lifestyle, try to walk whenever you can. If you live in a city that is walkable or full of parks and gardens, make the best use of it. If you're a busy parent and barely get time to yourself, participate in activities with your children as much as possible. You'll be surprised at the amount of physical activity you can get in this way.

- Be patient and celebrate your wins. It's understandable that you want to see results as soon as you start putting in the effort. Of course, your mind and body will start feeling different almost immediately. However, the first few days or weeks will likely be more about the soreness you experience or the resistance you deal with when adjusting to a more demanding regime than you're used to. Remember to breathe through all of this and celebrate your milestones, as small as they might seem to you. If you're able to get out of bed at six every morning, that's something to be proud of. Similarly, if you can walk one mile each day without feeling winded up, give yourself a pat on the back. You're choosing yourself every day, and that's a rare and brave thing to do.

Getting the Most Out of Your Exercise Routine

If you want to get the most out of your exercise routine, you need to ensure that your lifestyle supports your fitness goals. The most important aspect of this is your diet. If you're engaging in high-intensity workouts, it's very important to protect your muscles from injury and extreme wear and tear. A diet that includes adequate amounts of protein will help repair and grow your muscles. Wherever possible, try to get your protein intake from whole foods instead of supplements. Some of the best sources are fish, lean meats, eggs, cheese, yogurt, milk, whey protein, soy, and nuts or seeds.

Intense workouts also mean that you might need to increase your carb intake. However, make sure that you're consuming food that is nutritious and doesn't spike your blood sugar too much. It's a good idea to incorporate whole grains into your diet. Some foods that you can consume after a workout are fresh fruit, milk, oatmeal, quinoa, whole wheat bread, whole grain pasta, legumes, and sweet potatoes.

You might find your appetite increasing a bit when you start exercising regularly. This is a good thing, but try to satiate your hunger with whole foods rather than unhealthy snacks. Also, don't skip meals and eat at regular intervals. This will help boost your metabolism, which will help you achieve weight loss faster. An important part of a healthy diet is drinking water regularly. Since you tend to lose a lot of water (and even certain minerals) when you sweat, it's important to replenish your body by drinking water. This will help your muscles recover faster and also make it easier for you to build strength. If you want, you can also drink coconut water, lemon water, buttermilk, and different herbal teas. These would help replenish your body with different nutrients as well. As much as possible, stay away from carbonated and caffeinated drinks, as they can lead to dehydration.

Before you start your exercise routine, make it a point to warm up and stretch your muscles. This will help prevent injury and also increase the efficiency of your workouts. Similarly, it's a good idea to spend some time cooling your body down and settling your heart rate at the end of your routine.

In order to take proper care of yourself, you need to take regular rest days. If you want, you can still engage in light exercises like a short walk during this time. Be careful of overdoing your exercises, as it can set you back on your fitness journey. Your day of rest can also be spent in self-care, either through gentle massages or restorative practices that help your muscles to heal.

The most important thing to understand when it comes to physical activity is to allow your body to find its own rhythm and to have fun while you're at it.

THE IMPORTANCE OF QUALITY SLEEP

At the beginning of your health and wellness journey, you might find yourself doing everything right and still not getting the results you hoped for. You could be eating healthy food throughout the day and exercising regularly, but still feeling tired and dissatisfied on your journey. If you don't know what the issue is, there's a good chance that your sleep cycle isn't where it should be. Even though sleep is one of the most important factors that determine our overall health, it often goes overlooked.

If you're a busy professional, you might perpetually be struggling to get everything done in a day. It's no wonder you make do with the bare minimum sleep possible. However, regularly ignoring your sleep can come at a steep cost to your health. In this chapter, let's understand the importance of good quality sleep, the harmful effects of ignoring sleep, and ways in which we can improve our sleep schedule and quality.

Are You Getting Good Quality Sleep?

Sometimes, you might think that the cost of getting ahead in life is sacrificing sleep. However, good quality sleep is essential to your quality of life as well as your success. What exactly is good quality sleep? Since 1990, the National Sleep Foundation has been trying to research the benefits of proper sleep, as well as the health risks that come with inadequate or disturbed sleep. At different stages of our lives, we need different amounts of sleep. According to the National Sleep Foundation, this is the minimum amount of sleep that the average person requires at various stages:

- Newborns (0-3 months): 14 to 17 hours

- One- and two-year-olds: 11 to 14 hours

- Six- to thirteen-year-olds: nine to 11 hours

- Adults younger than 65 years: seven to nine hours

- Adults 65 years and older: seven to eight hours

In general, sleep ensures that our bodies get the rest they need, and it also helps in growth and development. Proper sleep also leads to better learning, a sharper memory, and stronger mental development. This is why kids need more sleep than adults since they're still growing and learning multiple new things each day. However, the number of hours you get is only one part of the picture. First, the timing is important. No amount of sleep you get during the day can make up for the sleep you get at night. This is because your body's natural circadian rhythm is aligned with the sunlight. So, you might be sleeping for hours during the day and still feeling fatigued most of the time.

Second, you need several uninterrupted hours of sleep each night. Even if you manage to sleep for ten hours but find yourself disturbed during most of that period, you won't feel refreshed and energized in the morning. So, sleeping with your phone or any other digital device beside you isn't the best idea.

Third, your sleep should be restful. This is related to the second point but goes one step further. If you're relaxed and free of anxiety *before* you go to bed, the quality of your sleep improves considerably. This is why you should be mindful of how you spend the last few hours before going to bed.

The Risks of Poor Quality Sleep

We know that poor quality sleep leaves us feeling tired, irritable, and unable to do our best the next day. Still, the problems related to poor sleep might be deeper than we imagine. Let's look at some of these issues in this section.

Poor sleep can increase the risk of obesity and lifestyle diseases.

In 2006, a paper was published in the *Archives of Internal Medicine*, in which the researchers tried to establish a link between rising BMI (obesity) and inferior quality of sleep among rural populations in the US. The results showed that people who slept eight hours on average were less likely to be obese, whereas those who slept fewer than six hours had the highest BMI among the participants (Kohatsu et al., 2006). This study corroborated the findings of other studies that had previously established a link between poor sleep quality and obesity in urban populations.

In 2008, a paper was published in *JAMA*, which investigated the link between poor sleep quality and coronary heart disease. It used the amount of coronary artery calcification in participants as a measure of future heart disease. The study concluded that adults who regularly slept less than six hours a night showed higher levels of coronary artery calcification (King et al., 2008).

A study published in the *Archives of Internal Medicine* in 2006 tried to understand if poor sleep quality can increase the risk of type 2 diabetes in the participants. The results proved that people who got less than five hours of sleep each day had a greater chance of developing type 2 diabetes (Knutson et al., 2006).

Poor sleep can impair the immune function of the body.

In 2003, a study was published in *Frontiers in Bioscience*, which tried to understand how poor sleep can affect our immune system. It concluded that the less sleep we get, the greater the chances of inflammation in our bodies. Inflammation is a natural phenomenon that occurs whenever our bodies are infected. However, acute (short-term) inflammation resolves after a few days. Chronic inflammation, on the other hand, occurs when the body turns on itself and begins to recognize everything as an attack. This can lead to a whole host of problems, especially in terms of autoimmune diseases. This study proved that poor sleep could interfere with our normal immune responses (Opp & Toth, 2003).

This was further corroborated by a 2009 study published in the *Archives of Medicine*. This study proved that previously healthy participants who suffered from poor quality of sleep were more susceptible to common colds, which indicated a suppression in their immune function (Cohen et al., 2009).

Since sleep prepares the body for disease prevention and control, it makes sense that poor sleep greatly affects our quality of life and can also negatively impact our longevity.

Poor sleep quality has a huge impact on our mental health.

The relationship between poor sleep quality and poor mental health is difficult to ignore. When we miss even one night of proper sleep, we wake up feeling irritable and fatigued. Imagine what days or weeks of poor-quality sleep can do to our mental health. While there's still more research to be done on this relationship, we have enough evidence to believe that this is a bidirectional relationship. This means that poor sleep quality can increase our risk of suffering from various mental health disorders, such as anxiety, depression, and bipolar disorder. At the same time, if we're suffering from mental health issues, it can severely affect our sleep quality. So, insomnia and disturbed sleep patterns can act as symptoms for deeper issues.

One of the possible explanations for this is that poor sleep quality generally amounts to disturbances in different phases of the sleep cycle, especially in rapid eye movement (REM) sleep. This is the phase in which we tend to dream and work through our emotions and memories. When this phase is disturbed, or when we don't reach this phase, there's a greater tendency for negative thoughts to persist in our brains. When this becomes a pattern, it starts to negatively affect our moods and mental health.

Many people who suffer from depression also tend to suffer from insomnia. Most of them also tend to sleep during the day, and some sleep for much longer than needed. These behaviors have traditionally been linked to depression, but it's only recently that researchers have started seeing poor sleep as a cause (rather than just a symptom) of depression. This also implies that if patients can improve their sleep patterns, there's a possibility of a reduction in their depressive symptoms.

Poor sleep quality can also exacerbate conditions like anxiety disorders, panic disorders, obsessive-compulsive disorder (OCD), and post-traumatic stress disorder (PTSD). One of the main reasons for this is that worry can lead to your brain being greatly aroused, which means that your brain is racing too fast and thinking all kinds of thoughts in a very short span of time. Most of these thoughts tend to be negative, especially if you've experienced trauma of some kind.

We've discussed before that good quality sleep means that our body is in sync with its natural circadian rhythms. This means that we should be up by sunrise and sleep as early as we can after sunset. When this doesn't happen, our mental health can suffer. An example of this is seasonal affective disorder, which occurs in places where a prolonged winter means that there's little to no sunlight for months. This can affect our body's natural alarm clock, leading to sleep disturbances, mood disorders, and even suicidal tendencies in certain extreme cases.

Now that we know how poor sleep quality can affect our mental, emotional, and physical health, let's look at some of the ways in which we can improve our sleeping patterns.

How to Ensure Quality Sleep

When it comes to ensuring quality sleep, you have more power than you think. By taking care of your schedule, eating habits, and environment, you can make sure that you get a good night's sleep. These healthy habits that help you sleep better are also termed "sleep hygiene."

Let's look at some of these habits:

- Honor your body's natural circadian rhythms as much as you can. This means that you should get up when the sun comes up (or as close to it as possible) and sleep by 10 or 11 p.m. at the latest.

This can be hard to do in the beginning, but our bodies are adaptable, and they recognize when their internal clocks are listened to.

- You also need to get as much natural light as possible during the day. Try to avoid artificial light if you can. If you can, try to get out and get some sun exposure during the day. If you can, you should also engage in sunbathing. In this, you expose your body to sunlight to soak in all its goodness. The best times for this are half an hour after sunrise and before sunset. It's a good idea to apply sunscreen to avoid the harmful effects of sun exposure. Also, you should not spend too much time in the sun. Even a little bit during the day will help you immensely.

- One of the biggest disruptors of our natural circadian rhythms is the blue light that emanates from our digital devices, especially at night. How many of us have a habit of staring into our phone screens or even laptops long after the lights have been turned off in the bedroom? We might not notice it at first, but blue light can lead to both delayed and disrupted sleep. So, get into the habit of turning off your devices for at least an hour or two before going to bed. Again, easier said than done, but your body and mind will thank you for it in the morning.

- As much as you can, stick to the same sleep schedule every day. I understand that some days are more challenging than others, and you might struggle to go to bed or wake up at your scheduled time. That's okay. However, don't let one bad day devolve into a bad week or month.

- If possible, try not to sleep at all during the day. Daytime naps do little to really energize you and might even take away from your ability to get a good night's sleep. If you have a hectic schedule and need to rest in between, train your body for short naps of 20-30 minutes. Sleeping erratically or too long during the day can mess with your body's sleep rhythms.

- Exercising during the day can also help in ensuring a peaceful night's sleep. Not only does exercise help relieve stress, but it can also help your body wind down in a healthy manner. Even if you don't dedicate your time exclusively to exercise, try to stay as active as possible during the day. Make sure not to exercise at night, as most exercises increase our heart rate and make us feel active, which can interfere with sleep.

- The less stressed you are, the better are your chances of falling and staying asleep during the night. Most of us turn to our digital devices to keep us distracted and engaged, but this can be disastrous for our sleep cycles. So, look for other relaxing activities that you can do. For example, you can spend some time reading a book that you enjoy. Or, you can play a board game or spend some time talking to the other members of your family. Taking a warm bath or applying essential oils to your pulse points can also help you relax before going to sleep. If you like, you can even meditate for five to ten minutes before going to bed. Some people find it relaxing to journal before they sleep, as it helps them write their thoughts down and stop obsessing over them.

- Your bedroom should have an environment conducive to sleep. For one, try not to work or eat on your bed. This lets your mind know that the bed is reserved for sleeping. Two, turn off the lights in your bedroom after a certain hour. Three, keep your bedroom free from noise and disturbance. Four, invest in a good mattress and pillow, as they can make a huge difference to your sleep quality.

- What you eat during the day can have a significant impact on your sleep cycle. Try not to eat a particularly heavy and/or spicy meal in the evening. Most experts suggest that we eat our last meal at least three to four hours before going to bed. Even if you feel like snacking, go for something healthy like a veggie stick or some nuts and seeds. Try to avoid processed and junk food throughout the day, but especially at night. This is because the body takes a lot of time and effort to digest such foods, and this can disrupt our sleep patterns.

- Melatonin is a hormone that has a great impact on our sleep cycles. There are certain foods that can help with melatonin secretion, such as eggs, warm milk, nuts, fish (especially salmon and sardines), goji berries, and tart cherries. If you need, you should consult your doctor and start taking melatonin supplements under their supervision. Some other supplements, such as magnesium, ginkgo, *ashwagandha*, and lavender, might also help improve your sleep quality.

- Be mindful of the amount and type of liquids you consume throughout the day, but especially at night. For one, try not to drink too much water an hour or two before going to bed. You should also visit the bathroom before sleeping so that you don't have to wake up in the middle of the night to pee. Two, reduce your consumption of alcohol, as it can disrupt the release of important hormones and also cause sleep disturbances. Three, stay away from stimulants such as caffeine, especially at night. If you want to have something relaxing, try to opt for an herbal tea like chamomile.

- If you're struggling with insomnia, and most of the above methods don't seem to work for you, see a doctor to rule out any other conditions. In some cases, poor sleep might be symptomatic of a mental health issue. In other cases, a condition such as obstructive sleep apnea (OSA) might be responsible for the poor quality of your sleep.

Sleep is instrumental in improving our physical and mental health, so it shouldn't be overlooked no matter how busy your life is. In the next chapter, we'll differentiate between sleep and rest and learn how to incorporate more rest into our daily routine.

BE SURE TO REST

Most of us use the terms "rest" and "sleep" interchangeably. This is because we believe that we can only get our rest through sleep. We try to fill every waking hour with some activity or the other, so it's no wonder that we're perpetually exhausted. In fact, many of us live on the brink of burnout because we don't know how to rest. Another reason why rest is misunderstood by the western world is that we haven't yet learned the value of "doing nothing." We want to make everything productive, including our downtime. This is also why rest becomes recreation, which is another term for a list of activities that might not be restful at all.

In this chapter, we'll understand how sleep and rest are different from each other, and we'll also learn about ways to get more rest throughout the day.

The Difference Between Sleep and Rest

Sleep is an advanced form of rest. When we sleep, our bodies and minds shut down almost entirely. This means that everything except our vital functions (those that are necessary for us to stay alive) ceases, and our bodies use this time to carry out all the necessary repairs. For example, if our muscles or tissues have faced any wear and tear during the day, this is a good time for them to repair themselves. Thus, a good night's sleep can help rejuvenate your body and mind.

In many ways, sleep induces an altered state of consciousness. At this time, you cannot make sense of your environment, nor are you involved in processing new information. Sleep has many stages, each of which has a role to play in taking care of our bodies and minds. When we sleep properly (at least six to eight hours for adults), we not only take care of our bodies but also allow our minds to strengthen themselves. During this time, we're usually in different stages of unconsciousness. The REM stage is particularly responsible for dreams, where we work through our memories and enhance our learning processes. As we've seen in the previous chapter, sleep is most effective at night. Also, it should be uninterrupted for several hours for us to get the maximum benefit out of it.

Rest, on the other hand, is an entirely conscious state of being. Even if you don't participate in any activity during this time, you're aware of your environment, and you can also be affected by it. You can take a rest at any time during the day, and it doesn't need to be uninterrupted or even of long duration. Also, while you should ideally be sleeping in a comfortable bed in relaxing surroundings, you can experience rest in any surrounding that suits you.

While the requirements for good quality sleep are almost constant for people of a certain age and life stage, the meaning of rest can differ widely among people. Some people like to rest by doing absolutely nothing, which is more difficult than we might think. Others like to engage in certain pleasurable mental or emotional activities while resting their bodies. Still, others engage their bodies in activities that rejuvenate them. So, rest is an extremely individual endeavor for most of us. What counts as rest for you might be boring or tiresome for someone else.

Rest does not move from one stage to another, unlike sleep. In fact, anything that lowers your stress levels and refreshes you for the tasks ahead of you can count as rest.

Why Should We Focus On Rest?

We might think that getting adequate sleep is enough when it comes to rejuvenating our bodies and minds. There are a couple of things to understand here. First, if you're not getting enough rest, there's a good chance that you're not getting proper sleep. Why so? Because rest keeps us calm during the day, in the midst of activity. When we don't get proper rest, we're usually frazzled and stressed, which hampers our sleep quality.

Second, rest brings joy to your life. Life shouldn't be all about work and labor. In the last few years, most of us have been pushed to the limit by the challenges that the world has thrown at us. We've had to re-evaluate everything in life, and most of us have experienced stress and anxiety in a way we've never known before. This is also why the word "burnout" has entered the lexicon for most populations in the last couple of years. Once, this term was used to denote the effect that a job environment had on people who were in caregiving professions. It has become eerily familiar to most of us as we learn to care for others and ourselves in a strange new landscape.

Most of us, when we're asked to slow down and rest, push back against it. We tell ourselves, and others, that we cannot *afford* to rest. I would argue that this is exactly when we should rest. When we're on the brink of burning out, we feel perpetually tired and uninspired. It's as if our lives have been stripped of all meaning and joy. When we allow ourselves to rest in ways that nourish us, we gently invite joy back into our lives.

Third, rest is also a form of reinvention. We tend to ignore periods of rest because our culture makes us believe that we're not doing anything worthwhile during this time. It's even worse if we want to rest by doing absolutely nothing during that time. However, when we rest properly, we give our bodies and minds a break needed to perform well. More importantly, we encourage ourselves to become more creative when we rest. Most of our lives are filled with overly stimulating activities. Our senses are almost clogged with excess information, which is why we sometimes feel tired even when we're technically on a break.

So, when we learn to rest properly, we meet a version of ourselves that is not overshadowed by the demands of the hyperactive and hyper-digital world. We get ideas that are ours, we interact with the world in a unique and original manner, and we learn to befriend ourselves again. The fact that you can experience this almost every day only makes it that much more powerful.

Fourth, rest helps us recover and relax on a regular basis. Why is this important? Think of the number of days and months you spend slogging at work, dealing with various frustrations at home, and holding on to your sanity by a thread—all because you get to enjoy a vacation for a few days or weeks. Most of us believe that we need to escape our current lives to enjoy ourselves. This thinking brings with it a whole set of issues. For one, most vacations aren't as relaxing as we want them to be. Two, even the best vacations come to an end, which means that we have to come back to the same life that we left behind. Three, the ability to take regular vacations is linked to privilege, which means that not everyone can afford them.

So, does this mean that true rest is limited to a privileged few? Not at all. In fact, this is an indicator that we might be looking in the wrong places for rest. What if rest isn't a luxury but a birthright? What if rest is afforded to anyone who can stop and breathe deeply for a few minutes each day? What if we experience rest on a daily basis in our everyday lives? What if, through a combination of creativity, inspiration, and imagination, we finally give "rest" the recognition it deserves in our lives?

What Are Some Ways of Experiencing Rest in Your Life?

As we've discussed earlier, only you can decide what helps you rest on a regular basis. However, there are certain activities that are useful for most people. Let's discuss some of them in this section:

- Look for things that you can do for 15-20 minutes almost every day. These things should refresh you, and they shouldn't take a lot of effort to do. In other words, look for activities that don't stress you out. For some people, reading a book during this time keeps them engaged. For others, this is the time to discover and listen to different kinds of music. Still, others want to spend this time away from their devices and as close to nature as possible.

- While watching movies or a series on the television or on your digital devices could also be a way to unwind, make sure that you don't start binging on them or that they don't distract you from work. Also, staring into a screen for leisure *after* having stared into a screen for work might not be the refreshing break you're looking for.

- When you are able, try to utilize this time to take a short nap. While sleeping for hours during the day isn't usually healthy, short naps can leave you energized and ready for the rest of the day. This is especially helpful if you have a busy and hectic schedule.

- When you work from home, or you have friends at your workplace, you can utilize your breaks to spend more time with them. Good conversations and laughter have the power to heal us in a really short amount of time. Even if you don't have people around you during your break, try to call a loved one and have a short conversation with them. It can be extremely therapeutic just listening to their voice.

- You can also use this time to indulge in certain self-care rituals. If you're at home, you can run yourself a warm bath or give yourself a relaxing foot massage. You can even book a session close to work if that's possible for you. Also, remember that you don't have to spend money to feel good about yourself. There are many relaxing things that you can enjoy for free. For example, even a 15-minute walk in a park or any green space can recharge and relax you.

- As a general rule, try to spend time in nature whenever possible. You can start your mornings by simply soaking in your surroundings and end your evenings with a light walk. It's even better if, during this time, you're unplugged from digital devices of any kind. Pay attention to the ways in which each of your senses engages with nature. If you have the time and opportunity, you can even go for hikes or treks every now and then. These activities help you bond with nature and also contribute to your overall health. Whenever you're spending time with yourself or with your family, try to be outdoors as much as possible. Nature is the best salve available to all of us for free.

- If you have a little more time on the weekend or during the holidays, try to develop an interest or hobby that fulfills you. If you love music, you could learn to play an instrument. If you're a foodie, you could start cooking some easy but comforting meals. If you like languages, you could start learning one. If you love reading stories, this could be an opportunity to start writing some of your own. Admittedly, some interests might require more effort than others. However, if the process of developing them makes you feel energized and gives meaning to your life, you should go for it.

- One of the easiest and quickest ways to relax is also one of the most overlooked. This is because while we're always breathing, we're almost never conscious of our breaths. However, this simple act of bringing our awareness to our breaths can be empowering and relaxing at the same time. If you're someone who's always busy and might not have time for a dedicated session, all you need to do is check in with yourself every now and then. When you check in, ask yourself how you're doing, and if you feel extremely stressed, take three to five long and deep breaths through your nose. This can help reset your mind and body and make you feel more in control of your emotions. There are some other techniques you could try, such as ujjayi breathing or box breathing. While an ujjayi breath (in which you form a constriction in your throat) energizes you, box breathing (in which you inhale, hold, exhale, and hold again for the same amount of time) is a great way to relax your body and sleep better.

- If you feel stress too often, you can also learn a simple technique where you check in with your body to understand how it reacts to stress. This is known as a body scan. It doesn't take more than 10-15 minutes, and it can be done anywhere. If possible, you can lie down while doing this meditation, or you can complete it while sitting as well. The important thing is to be relaxed and in a safe place. Close your eyes if you want. Feel your feet or your entire body touching the ground and stay in that sensation for some time. Then, as you inhale, bring your awareness to different areas of your body. Start with your toes and move up to the top of your head. When you inhale, pay attention to how that part of the body feels. Does it feel relaxed or tense? Try to locate the exact place from which this tension emanates. Now, as you exhale deeply, release this tension from that part of your body. When you do this meditation, you might feel surprised at the amount of tension that your body has been holding on to. By simply becoming aware of this, we take a step toward letting go of this stress.

- Another way to relax is through progressive muscle relaxation. In this technique, you focus on different muscle groups at a time. As you inhale, you consciously tense these muscles. As you exhale, you relax them. By building tension in your body and then releasing it, you'll experience stress leaving your body and your mind.

- If you can merge movement with mindfulness, you'll be able to relax and feel energized at the same time. Mindfulness consists of different practices that tether you to the present. Anything that helps you focus on the here and now can come under mindfulness. Just as mindfulness keeps your mind in the present, movement allows you to get out of your head and inhabit your body in beautiful ways. Together, they're extremely powerful in giving your health a much-needed boost. You can opt for any kind of movement, from walking and running to yoga and Pilates. Even if you don't want to enroll in a class or do something that resembles a workout, you can always let yourself loose and dance whenever you feel like it. You might be extremely self-conscious at first, but before you know it, you'll be moving to your own rhythm and connecting deeply with yourself.

- Visualization techniques are also a great way for you to relax, especially when you're unable to physically take a long break. As the name suggests, in this method, you simply visualize a place or a scenario that brings you comfort. For some, it could be a walk along the beach or a hike up the mountains. For others, it could be a memory from an amazing vacation you took some time ago. If you're living away from home or family, you could also visualize sharing a home-cooked meal with them. Anything that makes you feel warm and comfortable is a good idea. Of course, these places might bring up strong emotions within you. Try to avoid yearning for a place too much, as that might lead to frustration and stress. Use your imagination to feel happy and calm, as if you're already in that place or scenario.

- If you find yourself feeling restless or anxious frequently, it might be a good idea to seek professional help. A good therapist will help you understand your destructive thought and behavior patterns and also help you break out of them through techniques such as cognitive behavioral therapy (CBT).

In a world that frequently overwhelms and underwhelms us at the same time, it can be difficult to find our center. However, with time, patience, and tenderness, we can teach ourselves to rest and reconnect with the world within and around us.

FIND YOUR EMOTIONAL SUPPORT SYSTEM

Sometimes, it seems like a part of the American dream is to become so self-sufficient that you don't need anybody else in your life. In some ways, independence is a great gift. After all, any kind of independence—financial, social, and emotional—implies that we don't need anyone else to succeed in life. We're not codependent on others, and our mental health and happiness are not dependent on someone else. If you're independent, you can show up in your relationships as an attractive partner, friend, and parent. However, this concept is usually abused or taken to extremes in our culture.

In some people, this manifests as hyper-independence, in which they don't let anyone else share their emotional burdens. In most cases, this is because they're scared of getting too close to others or of depending on them. Maybe they've suffered trauma as children, or maybe they've never known what it means to feel safe and secure in someone else's presence. While it's great to be responsible for your own needs, it's not a weakness to admit that you might need to rely on someone from time to time.

In others, this quest for independence comes at the cost of community. Their lives become all about their work, their closest relationships, and their needs—so much so that they don't even realize how isolated they've become until something catastrophic happens and they need help from others. When the pandemic hit the world a few years back, people were forced into quarantine and isolation. Those of us who were already living away from our families or communities were hit the hardest, and most of us found it difficult to cope with the numerous challenges that we faced daily.

The thing is, independence and interdependence aren't mutually exclusive concepts. In fact, people who are independent in healthy ways can form mutually beneficial relationships with others without jeopardizing the relationships. If the last few years have taught us anything, it's that we're really not meant to live alone, trapped in our bubbles. We need others to survive, and we need them to build a world where care and community ensure the health and longevity of its people.

In this chapter, we'll understand why it's important to find your own community and how we can build our own emotional support system.

What Is an Emotional Support System?

Do you have someone to turn to when you're worried or anxious? Do you have someone to talk to about your concerns? Are there people in your community who can help lighten your load in practical ways? Are there people at work who can help you navigate the challenges of your career and offer you sound advice from time to time? If yes, then you already have a very strong emotional support system in your life. If you don't, this is the time to start thinking about creating one.

Benefits of an Emotional Support System

Having a strong emotional support system means that you're never lonely. This doesn't mean that you're overly dependent on others to fix your problems or that you don't enjoy or prefer solitude in your life. All it means is that when you need to connect with someone, you'll have the opportunity to do so.

In social situations, this means that you have people who support you. If you're a new parent, say, you might benefit from people dropping in to see if you need anything, preparing meals for you and your partner, and helping out when things get a bit overwhelming. If you're coming to terms with your identity, you need people who make you feel safe and seen during this time. Similarly, if you have any questions or doubts related to your life path, it might help to have a community elder guide you through them. It means having good friends to hang out with, of course, but it also means that you have the support of a community when things get tough.

In personal relationships, you should always be able to rely on your closest friends and family members. Some of these people could be there to listen to you at odd hours. Others could be extremely tolerant and non-judgmental when it comes to your life choices. Still, others could give you the tough love that you need every now and then. If you completely trust someone, they could even check in with you regularly to make sure you're doing well. When our personal relationships make us feel emotionally supported, they allow us to be vulnerable and intimate with others, deepening our connections in the process.

At work, having an emotional support network means two things. One, it helps you vent in a healthy manner when things get tough. All of us have those days when the crushing pressure gets to us, and we feel trapped. During these times, if you have people who'll lend you a sympathetic ear and understand what you're going through, it can help relieve some of the stress you're experiencing. Two, your emotional support at work can comprise people who you love working with or those who you want to work with. The aim is to learn from each other and to give and receive advice when needed. Of course, these people should also be trustworthy and respectful at all times.

Sometimes, we can also build communities with people based on shared interests or goals. For example, if you've decided to start practicing yoga, you can join an online or offline class in which you not only learn together but also keep each other accountable. Similarly, if you're trying to eat more plant-based foods but don't know where to start, you can meet people online who have made the transition and get inspired from them. Such groups also help when our usual support groups don't have people who align with our new goals or lifestyles. For example, if everyone you know loves eating meat, it might be challenging for you to feel motivated to stick to your new lifestyle.

When you find these people, you feel less lonely and stressed. Not only does this improve your mental and emotional health, but it can also have a positive impact on your physical health. When we have good emotional support systems, it increases the quality of our lives and also helps us live longer.

What Is Your Safe Space?

This world can sometimes make it very difficult for us to be our authentic selves. Most of us try to conform to the expectations that the world sets for us simply because we never know who we truly are. This is because it becomes practically impossible for us to find spaces where we can feel safe and understood. Most of us are too scared of judgment and betrayal to ever truly let our guard down. As the world becomes hyper-connected and perpetually online, it can become even more difficult to be our true selves. Before we know it, the masks we continuously wear can become indistinguishable from our personalities. So, it's now more important than ever to create a safe space for ourselves.

How to Build Your Safe Space?

If you're trying to build your community or safe space, there are a few things to keep in mind.

- The first thing to do is to understand what you need from the people around you. What are your goals in your career and relationships? Who are your role models? Are there any good examples of the kind of spaces you want to inhabit? Who are the kind of people missing in your life? Answering these questions honestly will let you know about the kind of connections you need to actively seek in your life.

- When you know what you need, look out for people who can offer you those things. For example, if you need a mentor at work, try to engage people in conversations to understand the right kind of leaders in your workplace. Similarly, look out for events at work that might help you connect with the right kind of people. When you network with a particular goal in mind, it can help you get better results.

- If you're someone who takes time to open up to people in a physical space, you can also consider joining an online community in the beginning. There are many online spaces where you can meet new people and start amazing conversations from the comfort of your home. If you're using social media to build your community, it's extremely important to make that space as safe as possible. Make sure that you don't get addicted to social media, and also ensure that the people in your community have similar goals as yours.

- If you live far away from family and friends, try to schedule regular meet-ups with them. You can split the costs of travel and decide to meet midway. Also, try to find people who live close to you, as all of us need people around us from time to time. You can also try to find ways of online and virtual communication with people who matter to you. For example, you could schedule a weekly Zoom call with your friends, or you could organize a virtual party for your family to commemorate an important event. For those of you who like written communication, you can even start an email group or a newsletter through which you can keep in touch with people who are interested in sharing their ideas and perspectives with you.

- If you're introverted by nature, it might take some time for you to build a safe space for yourself. However, you shouldn't see this as a drawback. In fact, it could be an opportunity for you to build more long-lasting and meaningful relationships. Having said that, it's not a bad idea to try getting out of your comfort zone every once in a while. Try engaging in any one activity that you wouldn't otherwise do, maybe once a month or even a quarter. You might end up surprising yourself and meeting some really interesting people in the process.

- It's also a good idea to keep reviewing your inner circle regularly. While we all need people around us who encourage us and make us feel good about ourselves, we also need people who keep us grounded, tell us the truth when we least want to hear it, and give us constructive feedback on our actions. So, make sure that you're not playing it safe and that you have people in your group who are both kind and honest. Ultimately, a safe space is possible only when all the members have each other's best interests at heart.

- Any kind of community or safe space only works when you give and take help in equal measure. If you're someone who hesitates to ask for help, get into the habit of doing so. I know it can be disconcerting to ask for help when you're used to taking care of yourself. However, asking for help isn't a sign of weakness. In fact, it takes a self-assured person to know their own worth and understand that asking for help will not diminish it. Also, you should try to offer help to other people so that you don't feel like you're taking advantage of someone else's kindness. A strong community is built on the understanding that every member has their unique strengths which can enrich the lives of others.

- If you want to build a truly safe space, you need to understand how to provide the help that others need rather than the help you think they need. It's important to ask the person what they might need at the time and see if you can offer that to them. Sometimes, this also means stepping back and letting them make their own decisions. Other times, it means offering them the best advice that you can think of. Knowing when to relinquish control in your relationships is key to building a safe space for others in your life.

- This last aspect is overlooked a lot of times when we discuss the building and sustenance of safe spaces. You need to learn how to set and maintain healthy boundaries with other people if you want your connections with them to remain strong and deep. When your boundaries are extremely rigid, you might have trouble being vulnerable with others or letting them open up to you fully. When your boundaries are loose, you might be giving too much of yourself and not getting enough in return. Healthy boundaries imply that you can say no when things get too overwhelming for you, you know when to step back and give others their space, and you can balance vulnerability with privacy. Without healthy boundaries, you might find yourself burning out and unable to provide anything of value to others.

Now that you've created your emotional support system, it's time to enrich your life by making the small things matter.

Learning to Enjoy Your Time

Most of us have our days crammed with all kinds of activities, yet we feel drained at the end of the day. Even the weekends and holidays go by in a blur, and we're left feeling empty and restless. This is because most of our days are about work and responsibilities, and we're so breathless from trying to keep up that we forget to have fun every once in a while.

One of the main reasons why enjoying our lives has become so difficult is that we're putting too much pressure on ourselves. Most of us have started treating fun and recreation as a chore to be completed. Even the activities that our kids engage in have become too commercialized or competitive for them to enjoy them innocently. When play starts resembling work, we're all doomed.

Another reason is that our culture places a lot of emphasis on consumerism, which means that if we get something too easily (or for free), we don't value it a lot. After all, we have to work hard to be worthy of the most basic things in life, so how can enjoyment be available to us for free? What happens, as a result, is that we miss out on the small but significant joys in our life.

Additionally, this society expects us to be productive at all times. After all, isn't that what capitalism is all about? If we don't show results regularly, if we don't progress in material terms, and if we're not constantly proving that we deserve to be a part of the system, we're made to feel like misfits. So, people keep slogging day in and day out to earn their place in society, and society itself starts to resemble a broken machine.

It's high time that we change the narrative and reclaim joy in our lives. In this chapter, we'll understand the importance of enjoying ourselves and learn how to steal moments of joy from our daily lives.

Why Is It Important to Focus On Enjoyment?

We know that life can become extremely monotonous if we don't enjoy ourselves regularly. However, this doesn't mean that you need to engage in mindless pleasure or distract yourself from your purpose to enjoy life. While pursuing pleasure for the sake of it can make you miserable, finding joy in your routine can add meaning to your life. What are some of the benefits of this?

- Even if your vocation is different from your passion, doing something you enjoy each day can help you become more productive. I know; it's ironic. The thing is, when our brains aren't constantly under pressure to perform, and when we do things that we enjoy, we let our brains relax. Without stress, our brains perform considerably better than before. So, it's always a good idea to spend some time doing absolutely "useless" things if you want to be more useful.

- There's no medicine like laughter. As I mentioned before, there's a slight difference between pleasure and joy. While pleasure is usually superficial and self-serving, joy comes from the way in which we connect with others. Even if we pursue joy in a solitary manner, we're still connecting to something deep within ourselves. This is more long-lasting than pleasure and certainly more healthy. So, joy helps improve our physical and mental health, gives us the strength required to face challenges, and helps us live longer.

- When we have fun on a regular basis, we give our brains a dopamine and oxytocin boost. Since these are feel-good hormones, our brains become almost addicted to the feeling we receive when we engage in these activities. In this way, we develop healthy and joyful habits for life. In a way, the activity is its own reward, so we don't need an external stimulus to keep repeating these behaviors.

- Since joy brings meaning to our lives, it keeps us from falling into a rut. When things are going wrong, or when life becomes mundane, these activities help us feel motivated. Amidst all the responsibilities that we need to fulfill, we're encouraged by the fact that we have something fun to look forward to during the day.

- When we're following the same routine day in and day out, our lives start running on autopilot. This isn't the kind of boredom that cultivates creativity but the kind that deadens our imagination. This is why it's recommended to try out something new every now and then. While this is great advice, it's also true that not everyone can afford (through time or money) to sign up for a new class every few months or travel extensively in a year. Is joy elusive to them? Not at all. In fact, we have the opportunity to understand what true joy means if we can only change our perspective. When we push ourselves this way, we challenge our imagination and give ourselves a fresh outlook on life. Needless to say, this also helps us become more creative.

- Without joy in our lives, both our work and personal lives suffer considerably. When we consistently feel stressed, anxious, angry, or sad, we cannot give our best selves to our relationships. Most of the anger and frustration we feel can spill over into our connections, rotting them from the inside. People who're well-balanced, happy, and peaceful are usually attentive partners and parents, empathetic friends, and kind strangers. Moreover, so many of these activities can be enjoyed with your friends and family members. When you seek joy together, you deepen your bond with your partner, child, parent, or friend.

Before we move on to ways of bringing joy into our lives, let's settle a question that has become extremely relevant these days.

Do You Need to Make Your Hobby Your Profession?

Let me start by saying that this question doesn't have a simple "yes" or "no" answer. Let's examine it from different perspectives. First, there are many factors that go into deciding whether your hobby should become your profession. The fact that you enjoy something is only part of that equation. You also need to consider whether you're actually good at it (at a professional level) and whether there's any real need for it in society. After all, if you're trying to make money from something, you need to consider its value in material terms. Don't be surprised if that takes away some of its charm.

Second, a profession requires many hours in a day to be dedicated to it, and not all of these hours are pleasant. After all, you're dealing with difficult clients, demanding supervisors, and your own team to present something that you can be paid for. Even if you enjoy the work, there's a good chance that you might not enjoy the stipulations that come with it.

Third, if you want to excel in a profession, you have to deal with competition. That's the only way to prove you worth. Of course, healthy competition can actually help improve your work and make you better at what you do, but if you're always thinking in terms of wins and losses, will you feel joy like you did before? Also, you're now considering whether you're "worthy" of doing something instead of simply doing it and enjoying yourself. This can easily take all the fun out of the process.

Fourth, some of us simply don't enjoy the circumstances necessary to pursue our hobbies and see where they lead us. This isn't to say that the path is easy for anyone. Except for people who might have certain advantages because of their influence and connections, most of us have to prove ourselves when we're converting our hobbies into our professions. However, some of us have it harder than others. For example, someone might be able to afford a few months off work while they're trying to figure out their career path, while others might not have that privilege. Similarly, people who have young children, need to take care of ailing parents, or simply have more familial responsibilities need to consider many things before they can take a step toward "pursuing their dreams."

Again, we have many examples of individuals who have persisted despite all odds, but it's worthwhile to acknowledge that luck and privilege play a huge role in making this path easier for some of us.

I'm not asking you to give up on your dream altogether. All I'm saying is that there needs to be a more nuanced discussion about this topic, and you should consider all the factors before making this leap. I'm also not saying that this is an easy path; you should expect struggles whenever you pursue something seriously. Still, it's important to ask yourself, "Am I still going to feel joy when this becomes my profession?" "Am I going to enjoy doing this for 10-12 hours each day, often without enough monetary compensation (at least in the beginning)?"

If you can choose joy each day in this endeavor, I say go for it. Otherwise, it's best to hold on to your hobby and find a few hours of relief and joy through it every day or week. Isn't that valuable in itself?

Finding Joy in Our Daily Lives

The path to finding joy is at once individual and collective. Since so many of the factors that keep us from actively pursuing joy are systemic, efforts are needed at the community, city, and country levels to make it easier for people to relax and enjoy themselves. Before these efforts are realized, however, the strength that we get from our communities can sustain us and make us enjoy the trivial things in life.

At an individual level, joy can be found in many ways—two of which are extremely important, in my opinion. One of them is through practicing gratitude daily. Another is by experiencing awe. Moreover, these two methods are dependent on each other.

Gratitude

When we're dealing with the constant pressures of our life, it's completely normal to forget how blessed we truly are. I'm not saying that we don't have real problems in our lives. Some of us must deal with a lot of challenges every day, and life's certainly not easy for most of us. When you practice gratitude, you don't forget your problems, nor do you see life through rose-tinted glasses. That wouldn't be very healthy, would it?

To be truly grateful, you need to be gracious. You need to acknowledge the challenges in your life, but you cannot let them make you bitter. In fact, each time you're able to overcome a challenge, you should be thankful for the strength and persistence you've been bestowed with. Each time you're able to share a laugh with your loved ones amidst a difficult time, you should be grateful for the ability to do so. Each time you look forward to the next day, despite being exhausted, you should be thankful for the grit you possess and the hope you've been given.

I would even argue that when things become really tough, that's when you should practice gratitude more than ever. There are some other misconceptions when it comes to gratitude. Some people believe that you need to be religious or spiritual to be grateful. After all, who are you grateful to if not a Higher Power? I believe that practicing gratitude can be seen as a spiritual act because it does nourish your soul, but it's much more than that. When you practice gratitude, your body and mind are also affected positively.

What's more, when you're expressing gratitude, you're saying "thank you" to everyone who makes your life easier for you. This could include your parents, who've raised you well and made you the person you are today; your partner, who's been by your side through all the ups and downs of life, and your children, who've taught you the meaning of unconditional love. This could include your friends who've accepted you at your worst and celebrated you at your best. In fact, this could even include strangers who've made your day easier with their service or kindness. If you don't take whatever you have for granted, you understand gratitude.

Another common misunderstanding is that you can only be grateful when something big happens in your life. For example, if you tell yourself that you can only truly be happy or grateful when you start earning a certain amount of money, or when you reach a certain milestone, you're effectively trapping yourself in a cycle of longing and frustration. Sometimes, we need to consciously look for the many blessings in our life. These small things will, in turn, pave the way for immense joy.

One of the best ways to start practicing gratitude is by keeping a gratitude journal. In this journal, you can note down the things that you're grateful for each day. It could be a kind word that someone said to you, or it could be the helpful neighbor who brought you food when you were sick. Of course, whenever you can, you should help others and pay it forward. If you've had a really bad day, you could be tempted to write nothing in your journal. I would suggest that you dig deeper on those days or simply pay more attention to your surroundings. For example, if you've had a terrible day at work but have come to a warm homemade meal, that's more than enough blessings for today.

Similarly, if you're worried about the future of your family and feel particularly helpless, spend some time with them (preferably outdoors) and cherish the moments that you're able to enjoy with them. When we make gratitude the focus of our lives, we learn to enjoy almost every moment of it.

Awe

Awe is a complex emotion that we experience when we're in the presence of something greater than ourselves. Though the feeling of awe doesn't always have to be positive, it does take us out of our mundane existence and makes us transcend our everyday life. For an emotion this huge, you might expect the experiences associated with it to be larger-than-life, too, right? After all, we're awed by people who have larger-than-life personalities. We feel awe when we're in the presence of a beautiful bird or an enormous animal. We're awed by events that we hadn't anticipated and those that change the course of our lives forever.

Since this emotion is one that we rarely experience and one that makes life more interesting, it makes sense that we chase this emotion. This is probably why some people love participating in adventure sports and feeling the adrenaline course through their veins. This is also why people want to visit new places on earth, preferably those that haven't been discovered yet, and those that remain outside the reach of most.

When people reach beyond their limits, and brave various difficulties in trying something new, the feeling of awe they get makes everything worth it. The question is, can all of us experience this feeling? Or is it limited only to a privileged few? The good news is that more and more researchers have become interested in the science of awe, and they're trying to understand how awe can be experienced in our daily lives.

The Greater Good Science Center at the University of California, Berkeley, is one such institution that has done extensive research in this field. The most interesting conclusion that they're reached is that we can all experience awe several times a day through simple techniques and behaviors.

One of them is—you guessed it—through regularly practicing gratitude. When we're grateful for the small things in our life, we elevate them to a level where they become important. Gratitude also makes us more observant and mindful in our daily lives, and this is the second thing that makes awe possible for us. When we become more attentive in our lives, we begin to connect deeply with nature. Nature, as it turns out, regularly gives us reasons to remain in awe.

So, you don't need to scale a mountain to experience awe. You can do so by simply feeling the wind against your skin. You don't need to be transported to a postcard-perfect village in a remote place on Earth. You can marvel at the rainbow that forms after a sudden downpour and experience awe.

It is, in fact, a clever idea to make a note of all the things that bring you joy. It could be the smell of your favorite breakfast in the morning. Or, it could be the sound of your favorite person giggling. You could find awe in the way the morning sunlight creeps into your room, or you could find it in the way the sky blushes a deep red at sunset. A simple ritual of spending weekends with your friends could bring you joy, and so could the time you get to spend with your favorite book on a rainy day.

These small joys carry a gentle weight to them, one that anchors you but doesn't burden you. All you need to do is look for them.

08

GIVE THERAPY A TRY

In recent times, therapy has gained much more acceptance among people than it did in the past. One of the reasons for this is that discussions around mental health have become more common in the last decade or so. Also, more and more younger people, including teenagers, are struggling with mental health issues. It's become clear that we need to have open and honest discussions about our mental and emotional health in order to deal with this crisis.

Another factor that might contribute toward this is that the scope of therapy has expanded in recent times.

Many people now understand that you don't need to be dealing with a full-blown mental health crisis to see a therapist. In fact, therapy can be very useful to anyone who seeks to understand themselves better and who needs guidance to figure out certain aspects of their life.

While there are some concerns around therapy, it's something that you can consider if you want some help on your mental and emotional wellness journey. In this chapter, we'll look at the reasons behind considering therapy and the different approaches to therapy that might help you.

When Should You Consider Therapy?

Only you can decide if therapy is something you might want to consider at a certain point in your life. That being said, this is a checklist that might help you make this decision.

- Are you unable to deal with certain emotions, such as anger, sadness, or guilt? All of us experience these emotions from time to time, but if they've become unmanageable or destructive, that's when you need to be concerned.

- Are you constantly feeling tired—physically, mentally, and emotionally? Do you think you might be experiencing symptoms of burnout?

- Are your emotional and behavioral patterns starting to affect your work, relationships, and life in a negative manner? Are you distancing yourself from your loved ones, feeling disconnected at work, and struggling to stay motivated in general?

- Have people close to you expressed concern about your mental and emotional well-being?

- Are you suffering from certain physical conditions that you feel might be connected to poor mental health? For example, your skin could be breaking out much more than usual, or you might be experiencing a lot of hair loss. You might be dealing with debilitating headaches, severe digestive issues, and extreme fatigue. While these symptoms could be linked to certain physical diseases, they could also be due to extreme stress, anxiety, or depression. In fact, if you've been dealing with a combination of two or more of these symptoms for some time, it's a good idea to consider therapy.

- Have you been having trouble sleeping? Have these issues persisted even after taking care of your lifestyle? Are you troubled by persistent nightmares when you sleep? Are you plagued by too many (often negative) thoughts when you should be sleeping?

- Have you been indulging in unhealthy and destructive coping mechanisms to deal with stress and anxiety? For example, have you been eating compulsively or binge eating a lot more than usual recently? Have you started smoking or drinking (or doing so excessively) to cope with the pressures of your daily life? Have you started engaging in other addictions and risky behaviors, such as gambling or doing drugs? Similarly, have your relationships been suffering because of codependency, obsession, or insecurity?

- Have you faced a sudden trauma or loss in your life? Are you unable to cope with grief, or are you trying to suppress the grief you're feeling?

- Do you want to understand your own patterns better? Do you want to free yourself from certain patterns that have become a part of your life? Do you want to resolve issues in your past so that you can move on from them and create a better future for yourself?

- Do you want to stop feeling helpless and anxious all the time? Are you looking for certain tools that can help you take charge of your life and make decisions that honor who you truly are?

- Do you want to discover your true purpose in life and move toward it with confidence? Do you want to improve your performance at work, change your career, or understand what makes you truly happy?

If you think this is a long and comprehensive list of questions, that's because almost everyone can benefit from therapy. If you have certain issues that you need to address, you can talk to a trusted therapist. If you feel a little unsure about the path ahead of you, therapy might be a good idea for you. If you want to do more work within yourself, a therapist can take you through the tools that might help.

How Can Therapy Benefit You?

Simply put, therapy usually includes talking to a trained professional about your thoughts, feelings, and behaviors in a safe and non-judgmental setting. Since the relationship between a therapist and their patient is marked by trust and confidentiality, it becomes easier for the patient to open up in front of them. Also, a skilled therapist knows how and when to ask the right questions and when to pull back and allow the patient to talk through their feelings.

Most of us feel comforted when we talk to a trusted friend, family member, or even co-worker. It's true that in many circumstances, simply talking to these people can help us a lot and make us feel less lonely. However, there are certain situations where it might be best to seek the help of a professional. Also, no matter how adept your loved ones might be in helping you cope, they're not in a position to maintain healthy boundaries with you at all times. So, these sessions might begin to affect them as well and also cause a strain in your relationship. So, consider visiting a professional if you can.

We're only now beginning to see how our mental health can affect almost every aspect of our lives. Since many mental health conditions might also present symptoms in our bodies, therapy can help us in taking care of our mental health as well. For example, counseling patients who are dealing with excess skin and gut issues can help improve their digestive and dermatological health.

While therapy itself can be costly, it can also prevent the healthcare system from being overly burdened. Proper therapy can prevent small mental health concerns from burgeoning into mental health crises. Since it can provide us with tools to understand ourselves, it also helps create a more resilient population that can bounce back from unexpected events.

Things to Keep In Mind While Starting Therapy

Therapy helps us become the best version of ourselves, but it's certainly not a miracle cure. It takes a lot of time, patience, and effort to get the best out of therapy. Most people expect too much from therapy in a very short amount of time, which is why they feel disillusioned or give up too soon. So, temper your expectations and be realistic about what you hope to achieve from these sessions.

You can find a therapist through several methods. You can ask your doctor for a referral if they think your physical symptoms can improve through therapy. You can also check if your university or workplace offers you free counseling sessions. Since cost can be a factor in considering whether you can go to therapy, look for non-profit organizations or charities that work in the area of mental health, and see if you are eligible for some free or low-cost sessions with a therapist.

If you're able to afford private sessions with a therapist, you can look for their information on certain local or national websites. You can even ask a friend or family member to refer you to someone, but make sure to do your due diligence before beginning your sessions. You should thoroughly research the qualifications of your prospective therapist and make sure that they have a current license under which they're allowed to practice in your state. Therapists also need to adhere to a strict code of conduct, so make sure that they haven't obtained any violations.

When you start your session, your therapist will likely ask you why you've opted for therapy. They could also ask you questions about your current and past life, and about some of the most important relationships in your life. They might also give you an idea of how the sessions would be structured. There are many different kinds of therapeutic approaches—such as mindfulness-based therapy, CBT, and psychoanalytic therapy—that your therapist might suggest to get the best outcome.

It's a good idea to talk about what you can expect out of these sessions, how committed you are to the entire process, and what you're expecting at the end of these sessions. Make sure that both you and your therapist are on the same page about this. Also, while you need to give time for the process to show results, you should be honest about how you feel in your therapist's presence. If, after a couple of sessions, you don't feel comfortable with them or you feel like your energies just don't match, you should move on to the next therapist. Sometimes, it takes time for you to find someone you're comfortable with, and that's perfectly okay. Don't tell yourself that therapy is not for you if your initial experiences aren't entirely satisfactory.

In the next chapter, we'll look at the importance of getting regular medical checkups.

DON'T FORGET YOUR MEDICAL CHECKUPS

Gone are the days when people used to consult doctors only after they had fallen sick. Today, with more and more people becoming conscious of their overall health, it is becoming common to meet with medical professionals throughout our lives. It's also becoming clear that many diseases that plague us today are treatable and even preventable if medical intervention occurs at the right time.

Importance of Regular Medical Checkups

People who understand the importance of maintaining their health, especially as they grow older, see medical checkups as an ongoing conversation between themselves and their doctors. Not only does this build trust between the two of them, but it also makes it easier for the doctor to understand when something might be wrong.

Despite the growing awareness, there are still some people who avoid going to the doctor as much as they can. For some, the concerns might be cost-related. Most employer insurance plans make provisions for regular medical checkups, and these should be taken advantage of. If you're self-employed, you should research the various options available to you and make an informed choice about the best provider for you. This will help keep the costs to a minimum and also prevent costs from racking up if you need treatment at a later stage.

Others might be tempted to self-diagnose their conditions, which is useless in most cases and even dangerous in some. While the internet can provide you with a lot of information, and it's not the worst idea to be aware of certain things before meeting with your doctor, you need to trust their professional advice when it comes to your health. Otherwise, you might miss out on some vital health-related symptoms, or you might work yourself up in a frenzy over nothing.

Most of us who skip these crucial visits, however, do so because we're overly optimistic. Now, we should understand that prevention is the best cure when it comes to many diseases. We should also have an idea that our lifestyles have exposed us to certain risk factors that make it more likely for us to develop comorbidities. This makes the pursuit of health more complicated than we would like it to be, but feigning ignorance will not help us.

Not only do regular medical checkups help improve our lifespan, but they also help us live a healthier life in general. Even if we end up needing treatment for certain conditions, early detection will save us from complications that can affect our quality of life even after surgery or treatment.

Common Tests That Should Be a Part of Your Routine Checkup

Before conducting your routine physical exam, your doctor will usually ask for or confirm certain information that could impact your medical history. This can include your age and your family history. This data can help your doctor understand if you're at an increased risk for certain diseases. After that, they'll usually measure your height and weight to calculate your BMI. This is a commonly used marker for obesity and related health conditions. Though there has been some controversy regarding the accuracy of this marker to assess health, it remains the most widely-used formula to determine whether you can contract diabetes, heart disease, or some cancers.

Two other factors that are almost always checked for adults are—blood pressure and cholesterol. The amount of (bad) cholesterol in your blood indicates the number of unhealthy fats that might lead to greater chances of stroke and heart disease. It's a good idea to get your blood cholesterol levels checked every four to six years once you're over 20 years old. Also, if you have a history of high cholesterol levels in your body, suffer from obesity, or if you have a family history of diabetes or heart disease, you might need to get checked more regularly.

When your blood pressure is too high, you're at a greater risk of heart disease and stroke. Even extremely low blood pressure can be a concern, especially if it causes you to experience dizzying spells every now and then. Anything higher than 130/80 puts you in the high-risk category, which means you should get your blood pressure checked more often. For others, it's a good idea to get yourself checked every two years after you turn 18.

Another common condition that most people above the age of 45 should regularly test for is diabetes. Through a blood sugar test, you can know if you have diabetes or if you're predisposed to suffer from it at a later stage. Again, if you have a family history of diabetes or if you suffer from obesity, high blood pressure, and/or high cholesterol, your doctor might ask you to take these tests sooner and more frequently.

In some cases, you might even have an option of engaging in a preliminary counseling session to assess your mental wellness.

Apart from these tests, there are several others that might be prescribed to you depending on your age, your family history, and your physical condition (including new symptoms). This could include checking your eyesight and hearing if needed, checking your skin for any visible changes (this is something you should check on your own regularly), and checking your hemoglobin levels (especially if you show signs of anemia or if you're regularly menstruating). If possible, you should also visit a dentist as regularly as you can because oral health is intricately linked to overall health.

If you're older than 65 years, you would likely be asked to get your bone density checked, as it rapidly depletes after a certain age. If you suffer from conditions such as rheumatoid arthritis or if you're underweight, you might have to get yourself checked sooner. The same applies if you've had hip surgery or if you've been taking steroids for a long time. Anything that can cause your bone density to weaken is a cause for concern, as it increases your chances of seriously hurting yourself.

Some common cancer screenings for women focus on the breast and cervix, while for men, the most common ones are for prostate and testicular cancers. Apart from that, most people should get themselves screened for skin and colon cancer, especially after a certain age. You should ask your doctor about self-examinations wherever possible and also get a sense of the age after which these screenings should be done regularly.

For women, doctors might also recommend certain tests that help assess menstrual and reproductive health, as well as for hormonal conditions such as polycystic ovary syndrome (PCOS). Since micronutrient deficiencies are also on the rise, some of us might need to get tested for the same.

Even though no one particularly enjoys a visit to the doctor, regular visits with someone you trust can save you from a lot of trouble in the future.

GENERAL HEALTHCARE TIPS

We've now come to the last chapter of the book. In this chapter, we'll be going over some other things that you should keep in mind to ensure your overall health and wellness. Most of these are common knowledge, but we still need to remind ourselves to pay attention to these aspects regularly.

Practice Safe Sex

Sexual wellness is a huge part of our overall health. The first thing to remember is to get yourself tested for sexually transmitted infections (STIs) such as syphilis, gonorrhea, and HIV. If possible, try to minimize having sexual intercourse with too many strangers, as you're likely not aware of their health status. Minimizing the number of partners we have sex with can also help reduce the risk of contracting dangerous and potentially fatal diseases. Always use protection—whether through pre-exposure prophylaxis (PrEP), condoms, or dental dams. Remember that STIs can also be transmitted during oral sex, so keep yourself and your partner protected at all times.

Get Yourself Vaccinated

Vaccinations help strengthen the immune system of our body, thus preventing it from contracting a wide range of infections and diseases. Most of us have seen firsthand the life-saving capabilities of vaccines during the COVID-19 pandemic. Other diseases that vaccines can protect you from include hepatitis A, hepatitis B, measles, influenza, pneumonia, typhoid, polio, rabies, and yellow fever. If you have children, make sure that they've received their mandated vaccinations on time.

Be Responsible With Antibiotics

Many of us have gotten into the habit of self-medicating, especially when it comes to the more common bacterial or viral diseases. This is potentially dangerous and can cause unintended side effects in many cases. Also, if we keep taking antibiotics when they're not needed, we're going to develop antibiotic resistance. This means that future doses of the same antibiotic might not help combat a disease with the same efficacy as before. So, always consult your doctor before taking antibiotics, and make sure that you stick to the course prescribed by them. Don't share your antibiotics with someone else in the family, don't prescribe medications to others, and don't stop your medications before their course is complete. All of these actions can have negative consequences on your health and others.

Pay Attention to Your Physical Hygiene

It's become more important than ever to be mindful of your hygiene at all times. For this, you should take a bath once daily (and twice if needed), brush your teeth twice, and make sure you clean yourself thoroughly after coming home. You should be even more careful if you regularly interact with a lot of people or if you're a frontline worker.

In general, it's a good idea to clean your hands as regularly as possible. You can carry an alcohol-based sanitizer if you are traveling, or use soap if you're at home. If you're suffering from a cold, a cough, or other flu-like symptoms, you should consider wearing a mask in public. In any case, use your elbow to sneeze or cough so that you prevent harmful bacteria and viruses from spreading to others.

Another way in which we can stop bacteria and viruses from spreading is by ensuring that the food we cook and eat is hygienic. For this, you should always thoroughly wash your fruits and vegetables, and use clean water for cooking food. Also, if you're handling poultry, you should wash your hands as frequently as possible. Be aware of the temperature at which food begins to break down or rot. Also, keep cooked food separate from raw food, and make sure that all foods (especially those containing animal products) are cooked properly.

In general, the more control you have over the food you eat (more home-cooked meals), the more your chances of staying healthy.

Mental Health Is Important Too

Just as you should take care of your physical hygiene daily, you should also put aside a few minutes to take care of your mental health. During this time, you should be honest with yourself about the struggles you're facing at the time. For example, you could be dealing with too much stress at work. Or, you could be feeling anxious because of the changes that are happening in the world around you. Once you're aware of your challenges, you should think about the activities that could help improve your mental health.

For example, you could start a daily 10-minute meditation practice, or you could incorporate more mindfulness into your daily routine. You could also increase your level of physical activity to improve your mood during the day.

You should continuously check in with yourself to see if your activities are impacting your mental health positively. It also helps to create a circle of trusted friends and family members with whom you can openly talk to about your mental health and who can also encourage you to see a professional should the need arise.

These tips will help you stay safe and keep your loved ones safe for a long time to come.

CONCLUSION

Even as we realize the importance of holistic health and wellness, we feel more overwhelmed by the day when it comes to making practical changes to our lives. This is the conundrum that most of us face today, and it's something that I've grappled with for a long time.

I realized that, instead of hope, most of us feel dread when we need to make decisions about our health. Instead of feeling empowered, we feel powerless. Instead of enjoying our lives to the fullest, we spend most of our time worrying about our health.

I also realized that we need to stop overcomplicating our health and wellness journey. There are some basic principles that we need to follow if we want to enjoy good health for the rest of our lives. When I started this journey, I was unsure of the results. However, once I saw the impact that these changes had on my health, I promised myself that I would help others who were struggling on their wellness journey. This book is a result of that promise.

Some of the things we learned in this book are

- We need to make better and more informed food choices so that we get the proper nutrition we need.

- With this in mind, we should pay attention to nutritional recommendations and also learn to read food labels when we go shopping for groceries.

- There are certain things that we should consume less than we usually do, namely, salt, sugar, proteins, and highly processed food.

- When it comes to supplements, it's best to err on the side of caution. If you have to take a supplement, make sure to consult with your doctor first.

- The more active we are during the day, the better it is for our mental, emotional, and physical health.

- There are many different forms of physical activity that we can choose from, and each has its own benefits. We should take some time before we come up with an exercise regimen that suits us.

- Sleep is a powerful but underrated aspect of good health. As important as it is to get the required number of hours of sleep at night, it's equally important to ensure the quality of our sleep.

- Even though rest and sleep are often used interchangeably, they're two separate states of existence. Rest has its own benefits, and there are many ways in which we can rest throughout the day. In fact, the more rested we are during the day, the better our chances are of getting good quality sleep at night.

- If we want to enjoy good overall health, we need to focus on our emotional health as well. For this, we need to seek out our emotional support systems and create a safe space for us to express ourselves authentically.

- We also need to nurture ourselves from within, and one of the best ways to do this is by enjoying ourselves to the fullest. We can do this by practicing gratitude on a regular basis, experiencing awe and joy through the smallest things, and engaging in hobbies that enrich us.

- Even if we're in control of our emotional and mental health, we might still benefit from therapy. It's important to know why you're seeking therapy and also to research properly before selecting a therapist to work with. When done well, therapy can lead us to excellent insights about ourselves and help us reach our potential in life.

- No matter how fit and healthy you might look and feel, it's important to consult with your doctor and get yourself tested regularly, especially after a certain age. The aim is to prevent any major issues from arising or to minimize the damage in case there is an illness.

I hope that this book has given you the encouragement you need to take control of your health and wellness journey. I wish you all the very best for the sometimes challenging but always rewarding journey ahead.

REFERENCES

Abbreviations Your Doctor Uses. (n.d.). WebMD. https://www.webmd.com/a-to-z-guides/ss/slideshow-useful-medical-abbreviations

Added Sugar. (2023, February 2). The Nutrition Source. https://www.hsph.harvard.edu/nutritionsource/carbohydrates/added-sugar-in-the-diet/

Awe Definition | What Is Awe. (n.d.). Greater Good. https://greatergood.berkeley.edu/topic/awe/definition

Benefits of Healthy Eating. (2021, May 16). Centers for Disease Control and Prevention. https://www.cdc.gov/nutrition/resources-publications/benefits-of-healthy-eating.html

Benefits of Physical Activity. (2022, June 16). Centers for Disease Control and Prevention. https://www.cdc.gov/physicalactivity/basics/pa-health/index.htm

Body Scan Meditation (Greater Good in). (2023, February 22). Greater Good in Action. https://ggia.berkeley.edu/practice/body_scan_meditation

Center for Food Safety and Applied Nutrition. (2022, February 25). *Sodium in Your Diet.* U.S. Food And Drug Administration. https://www.fda.gov/

food/nutrition-education-resources-materials/so-
dium-your-diet

Cohen, S., Doyle, W. J., Alper, C. M., Janicki-Deverts, D., & Turner, R. B. (2009). Sleep Habits and Susceptibility to the Common Cold. *Archives of Internal Medicine, 169*(1), 62. https://doi.org/10.1001/archinternmed.2008.505

Community, Y. S. (2016, August 26). *Why turning your passion into a career is terrible advice.* YourStory.com. https://yourstory.com/2016/08/turning-passion-into-career

Cronkleton, E. (2020, June 15). *11 Steps to Follow for a Post-Workout Routine That Gets Results.* Healthline. https://www.healthline.com/health/exercise-fitness/what-to-do-after-working-out

Day Designer. (2022, July 1). *Why You Need to Do Something You Love Every Single Day.* https://daydesigner.com/a/blog/why-you-need-to-do-something-you-love-every-single-day

Divanshi, G. (2022, May 28). *Difference Between Sleep and Rest (with Comparison Chart).* Bio Differences. https://biodifferences.com/difference-between-sleep-and-rest.html

Exercise: 7 benefits of regular physical activity. (2021, October 8). Mayo Clinic. https://www.mayoclinic.org/healthy-lifestyle/fitness/in-depth/exercise/art-20048389?reDate=11022023

Fitness program: 5 steps to get started. (2021, December 16). Mayo Clinic. https://www.mayoclinic.

org/healthy-lifestyle/fitness/in-depth/fitness/
art-20048269?reDate=11022023

Good Sleep Habits. (2022, September 13). Centers for Disease Control and Prevention. https://www.cdc.gov/sleep/about_sleep/sleep_hygiene.html

Healthy diet. (2020, April 29). World Health Organization. https://www.who.int/news-room/fact-sheets/detail/healthy-diet

Holcombe, M. (2022, April 25). *How 15 minutes of mental health hygiene can change your whole day.* CNN. https://edition.cnn.com/2022/04/25/health/mental-health-hygiene-wellness/index.html

Hood, J. B., PhD. (2022, July 26). *Importance of a Support System | Highland Springs Clinic.* Highland Springs. https://highlandspringsclinic.org/the-benefits-and-importance-of-a-support-system/

How To Read Food and Beverage Labels. (n.d.). National Institute on Aging. https://www.nia.nih.gov/health/how-read-food-and-beverage-labels

Integris Health. (2021, April 16). *Why It's Important to Allow Yourself to Rest.* https://integrisok.com/resources/on-your-health/2021/april/why-its-important-to-allow-yourself-to-rest

King, C. R., Knutson, K. L., Rathouz, P. J., Sidney, S., Liu, K., & Lauderdale, D. S. (2008). Short Sleep Duration and Incident Coronary Artery Calcification. *JAMA, 300*(24), 2859. https://doi.org/10.1001/jama.2008.867

Knutson, K. L., Ryden, A. M., Mander, B. A., & Cauter, E. V. (2006). Role of Sleep Duration and Quality in the Risk and Severity of Type 2 Diabetes Mellitus. *Archives of Internal Medicine, 166*(16), 1768. https://doi.org/10.1001/archinte.166.16.1768

Kohatsu, N. D., Tsai, R., Young, T., Vangilder, R., Burmeister, L. F., Stromquist, A. M., & Merchant, J. A. (2006). Sleep Duration and Body Mass Index in a Rural Population. *Archives of Internal Medicine, 166*(16), 1701. https://doi.org/10.1001/archinte.166.16.1701

Mackey, M. (2022, September 27). *100 Quotes About Self-Care, Because Being Good to Yourself Has Never Been More Important.* Parade. https://parade.com/1070248/maureenmackey/self-care-quotes/

Madeson, M., PhD. (2022, November 18). *The Importance of Counseling: 14 Proven Benefits of Therapy.* PositivePsychology.com. https://positivepsychology.com/why-counseling-is-important/

Mawer, R. M. (2020, February 28). *17 Proven Tips to Sleep Better at Night.* Healthline. https://www.healthline.com/nutrition/17-tips-to-sleep-better

May, K. (2021, October 19). *The Importance of Fun: Why having "Fun" is just as important as "Productivity."* Creative Healing. https://creativehealingphilly.com/blog/the-importance-of-fun-why-having-fun-is-just-as-important-as-productivity

Mueller, S. (2020, February 3). *80 Little Things in Life That Make You Happy.* Planet of Success. http://www.planetofsuccess.com/blog/2016/little-things-in-life/

Nutrition. (2019, October 11). World Health Organization. https://www.who.int/health-topics/nutrition

Opp, M. R., & Toth, L. A. (2003). Neural-immune interactions in the regulation of sleep. *Frontiers in Bioscience, 8*(4), d768-779. https://doi.org/10.2741/1061

Pomona Valley Health Centers. (2017, April 7). *The Importance of Regular Check-Ups.* https://mypvhc.com/importance-regular-check-ups/

Relaxation (n.d.). Mind. https://www.mind.org.uk/information-support/tips-for-everyday-living/relaxation/relaxation-tips/

Relaxation Techniques for Health. (n.d.). NCCIH. https://www.nccih.nih.gov/health/relaxation-techniques-what-you-need-to-know

Rico-Campà, A., Martínez-González, M. A., Alvarez-Alvarez, I., Mendonça, R. D. D., De La Fuente-Arrillaga, C., Gómez-Donoso, C., & Bes-Rastrollo, M. (2019). Association between consumption of ultra-processed foods and all cause mortality: SUN prospective cohort study. *BMJ,* l1949. https://doi.org/10.1136/bmj.l1949

Rosa, C. D. (2023, January 31). *Why you need an emotional-support network at work.* Work Life by Atlassian. https://www.atlassian.com/blog/teamwork/emotional-support-at-work

Scott, E. (2021, January 10). *How to Create Your Own "Safe Space."* Verywell Mind. https://www.verywellmind.com/how-and-why-you-should-create-a-safe-space-for-yourself-3144981

Sleep and Health | Need Sleep. (n.d.). Harvard Medical School. https://healthysleep.med.harvard.edu/need-sleep/whats-in-it-for-you/health

Smallen, D. (2022, July 29). *Connecting with others improves mental health, here's how.* World Economic Forum. https://www.weforum.org/agenda/2022/07/mental-health-connection-psychology-relation-ships

Srour, B., Fezeu, L. K., Kesse-Guyot, E., Allès, B., Mé-jean, C., Andrianasolo, R. M., Chazelas, E., Des-chasaux, M., Hercberg, S., Galan, P., Monteiro, C. A., Julia, C., & Touvier, M. (2019). Ultra-processed food intake and risk of cardiovascular disease: prospective cohort study (NutriNet-Santé). *BMJ*, l1451. https://doi.org/10.1136/bmj.l1451

Suni, E. (2023, February 9). *Mental Health and Sleep.* Sleep Foundation. https://www.sleepfoundation.org/mental-health

The Wellness Society. (2023, January 6). *What Is Therapy and How Does It Work?* The Wellness Society | Self-Help, Therapy and Coaching Tools. https://thewellnesssociety.org/what-is-therapy-and-how-does-it-work/

Theodore, N. (2016, April 7). *The Perspective Shift That'll Totally Transform Your Self-Care Practice.* Mindbody-green. https://www.mindbodygreen.com/arti-cles/mindfulness-is-the-secret-to-effective-self-care

Top 5 Supplements for Optimal Health: Stamford Spine: Chi-ropractic. (n.d.). https://www.stamfordspine.com/blog/top-5-supplements-for-optimal-health

Troy, D. (2021, April 2). *Healthy Sleep Habits*. Sleep Education. https://sleepeducation.org/healthy-sleep/healthy-sleep-habits/

20 health tips for 2020. (2019, December 31). World Health Organization. https://www.who.int/philippines/news/feature-stories/detail/20-health-tips-for-2020

Wempen, K. R. (2022, April 29). *Are you getting too much protein?* Mayo Clinic Health System. https://www.mayoclinichealthsystem.org/hometown-health/speaking-of-health/are-you-getting-too-much-protein

What is good sleep and how much do I need? (2022, June 2). www.heart.org. https://www.heart.org/en/healthy-living/healthy-lifestyle/sleep/what-is-good-sleep-and-how-much-do-i-need